THINKING

DIFFERENTLY

Digital Society

Reimagining Society for the Digital Era

Mohammad J. Sear

"Visionaries imagine and create new realities by challenging and disregarding the status quo..."

Mohammad J. Sear

First Edition Author: Mohammad J. Sear

Edit and Design: Publishing Spot

Publisher: Mohammad J. Sear

ISBNs:

• Ebook: 978-969-9092-01-5

• Paperback: 978-969-9092-02-2

• Hardcover: 978-969-9092-03-9

Author's Website: https://mjmsear.com/

Table of Contents

PREFACE

We are living in an unprecedented period, one that is commonly referred to as The Digital Era. This is not a mere technological shift; it is a fundamental rewiring of our existence, a deep and often unsettling transformation of how we work, connect, govern, and simply *be*.

The velocity and scale of this change are without parallel. While the agricultural and industrial revolutions unfolded over centuries and generations, the digital revolution is compressing a civilizational transformation into the span of a single lifetime. This acceleration creates a profound sense of disorientation, a feeling that our old maps no longer describe the new territory we inhabit. It is this unique challenge—the need to navigate a world that is changing faster than we can make sense of it—that necessitates a new framework for thinking about the future.

I believe Artificial Intelligence (AI), and particularly generative AI and agentic AI are the biggest disrupters of the digital era that we are living in today, and this book which has been developed by leveraging these technologies is a living proof of this disruption.

The purpose of the series of these books is to provide such a framework for nations to navigate this transformation not as passive observers, buffeted by the winds of technological change, but as active architects of their future.

The first book in this series focused on the critical importance of digital governance, arguing that a reimagined, digitally native governance model is the foundational element upon which a successful digital nation must be built. Without a government for example, that is itself not fluent in the language and logic of the digital age, any broader societal transformation will be built on sand.

But a reimagined nation cannot serve a society that remains tethered to analog-era assumptions, values, and structures. A digital government and broader governance model and a digital society are inextricably linked; one cannot truly succeed without the other. This book, therefore, turns our attention to the second, and arguably more complex, pillar: the **Digital Society**.

The transition to a Digital Society is a concept that is frequently misunderstood, often reduced to a simple metric of internet penetration or the number of citizens with a social media profile. This is a dangerously simplistic view.

A true Digital Society is a social system where individuals engage, connect, and fulfill everyday needs through digital means, but it is far more than the sum of its technological parts.

It represents a fundamental shift in how people interact, a new architecture for how they access and process information, how they form communities, and how they participate in civic life. It requires a purposeful, and often difficult, redesign of our social systems, our values, and our institutions to ensure they are inclusive, accessible, and resilient in a hyper-connected world.

The purpose of this book is to explore how we can thoughtfully and deliberately build a Digital Society that serves all its members. To do so with the necessary clarity, this exploration must be brutally honest about the perils we face.

The path to a Digital Society is not a utopian march toward progress. The same tools that can foster unprecedented unity and collaboration can also amplify division and hatred. The same data that can create deeply personalized and proactive services can also enable pervasive surveillance and control. The same platforms that give voice to the voiceless can also become conduits for misinformation that erodes the very foundations of public trust.

To navigate these high-stakes trade-offs, this book adopts the stance of an intellectual sparring partner. Its goal is not to provide simple answers or utopian blueprints, but to challenge our assumptions and test our reasoning.

Throughout these chapters, the "skeptic's voice" will be intentionally introduced to rigorously question the very propositions I put forward. If we are to forge a viable path through this complex new world, we must prioritize honest critique over easy consensus. The path forward is not a simple one, and it is paved with difficult choices and profound ethical dilemmas.

If there are three things I would like you to take away from this book, they are these:

"REIMAGE to TRANSFORM,"

"UNLEAR to LEARN,"

and finally be "PURPOSE DRIVEN."

These are not mere slogans to be printed on conference banners; they are essential disciplines for the journey ahead. They represent the intellectual toolkit required to dismantle outdated assumptions, to challenge the status quo, and to build a society that is not only digital but also just, equitable, and truly human.

To reimagine is to refuse the limitations of the present.

To unlearn is to have the humility to admit that our old maps no longer describe the new territory.

And to be purpose-driven is to ensure that in our rush to build the future, we do not forget why we are building it, and for whom.

About the Author

Mohammad J. Sear is a digital era futurist and thought leader, and is focused on bringing purpose to the benefits of the digital era for nations. He likes to think of himself as a Chief Disruption Officer. He has obtained leadership training from the Harvard Kennedy School of Government, USA and holds an MBA from the University of Leicester, UK. He is the author of the book "Becoming Digital Nations – reimagining countries for the digital era".

After a successful 12+ years career in the UK government during the premiership of Margaret Thatcher, John Major and Tony Blair, Mohammad moved to the private sector and has now for 20+ years been advising government, public and private sector organizations in the UK, Middle East, Africa, Australasia and South Asia on strategic challenges and digital transformation.

He is currently leading the Digital Government & Public Sector and Start-up practices across the Middle East and North Africa for a global consultancy firm, and in the past for a 3 year period he was also a Digital Government, Public Sector and Innovation lecturer at the Paris School of International Affairs, Sciences Po, France.

He is a catalytic public sector changemaker and champion of diversity & inclusion, and passionate about transforming government. Being a change agent with a bias towards action he has enabled governments to become more citizen-centric and achieve operational breakthroughs by harnessing conventional and digital capabilities, as well as leveraging the power of design thinking, agile, behavioral science, emerging technologies such as artificial intelligence.

He is sought after by senior leaders' in government, public and private sectors for his futuristic and strategic thinking, and surgical advisory capabilities.

As a thought-leader and author of publications in the areas of digital nations, society, economy and governance, citizen centricity, customer experience, service design & delivery, emerging technologies Mohammad is frequently requested to speak, moderate or be a panel member at top tier global events on topics including but not limited to: digital nations, emerging technologies, future of governance, humanizing technology, exponential digital transformation in countries, cross sector collaboration, citizen-centered governance, and design thinking in public policy.

Some of the articles he has authored include:

- Digital is great but exclusion isn't – make data work for driving better digital inclusion published in Harvard Business Review
- Holistic Digital Government published in the MIT Technology Review
- Want To Make Citizens Happy - Put Experience First published in Forbes Middle East

And others such as "Bringing Purpose to Digital in Government", "How Digital is Changing the Way We Listen to Customers", "How Can GCC Governments Sustainably Deliver Better Citizen Experiences", "What is the Cure for a Better Patient Experience in the GCC", "Application of the Global Star Rating System for Public Services".

Moving from insights to execution Mohammad has designed transformational initiatives in several areas such as GovTech and Innovation Labs, digital product accelerators, digital government transformation, digital government service models and national citizen experience measurement strategies.

Part I:

The Foundational Shift: From Faster Horses to New Worlds

Chapter 1:

Beyond Connectivity: Defining the Digital Society

The journey to becoming a Digital Nation, I have argued, requires a radical paradigm shift in our thinking. It is a call to move beyond the incremental, timid question:

"How can technology help our existing government operate more efficiently?"

And to embrace the transformative, audacious one:

"How should our country evolve to operate and thrive in the Digital Era?".

The former is a question of optimization, of patching a legacy system; the latter is a question of re-invention, of designing a new one.

This distinction is not a mere semantic preference; it is the central strategic choice facing every leader in the 21st century, and the gravitational pull towards optimization is immense.

Optimization feels rational. It is the language of management consultants and budget officers. It presents itself as pragmatic, measurable, and politically safe. It involves digitizing existing forms, automating established bureaucratic workflows, and bolting new software onto old institutional structures.

The result is a government that may be marginally faster or cheaper, but which remains fundamentally unchanged in its logic and its relationship with the citizen. It is the faster horse, an impressive biological specimen perhaps, but an evolutionary dead end in the age of the internal combustion engine.

The Political Economy of Optimization

The preference for optimization is not just a failure of imagination; it is a calculated political choice. Optimization delivers visible, short-term "wins" that are easily communicated to the public—a new government app, a website redesign, a reduction in processing times.

These are the currency of press releases and political campaigns. They create the appearance of progress without threatening established power centers, disrupting incumbent industries, or requiring the arduous, politically costly work of legislative reform. Re-invention, on the other hand, is inherently disruptive. It questions budgets, challenges departmental remits, and renders entire job categories obsolete, creating powerful internal and external opposition. Optimization is thus a form of political theater, a way to be seen as "modernizing" while ensuring that the fundamental distribution of power and resources remains untouched. It is the path of least political resistance, and for that reason, it is the default path to mediocrity.

The allure of optimization also lies in its calculability. We can project the ROI of automating a permit application process. We can quantify the efficiency gains of a new database system. Re-invention, by contrast, is unsettling, unpredictable, and politically fraught. It offers no simple spreadsheets, only complex, contested visions. It requires questioning the very purpose of our institutions. It asks not how to create a digital version of the Department of Motor Vehicles, but why, in a world of secure digital identity, verifiable credentials, and autonomous mobility, we need such a department at all. This path recognizes that true transformation does not come from applying new tools to old tasks, but from redesigning the tasks themselves, and often, eliminating them entirely.

To embrace this re-invention is to swim against the powerful currents of organizational and human psychology. Organizations, particularly large public sector bureaucracies, are governed by path dependency. The choices of the past constrain the possibilities of the present. They are also, quite naturally, governed by loss aversion; the perceived risk of a failed transformation looms far larger than the potential rewards of a successful one. The incentive structures reward stability and punish disruptive failure, creating a culture that systematically favors the known quantity of optimization over the profound uncertainty of re-invention.

This transformative thinking, therefore, cannot be a casual undertaking. It must be a disciplined practice guided by three core principles that serve as our compass: **REIMAGINE to TRANSFORM**, **UNLEAR to LEARN**, and be **PURPOSE DRIVEN**.

REIMAGINE to TRANSFORM

This is the mandate to escape the gravity of the present. It is the most difficult work, for our imaginations are themselves products of the very analog world we seek to transcend.

We must have the courage to imagine a future that is not merely a linear extension of the past. To do this requires looking at historical precedents for transformations of this magnitude. Consider the invention of the printing press.

It did not simply make the production of hand-copied Bibles more efficient. It shattered the very foundations of a society built on information scarcity. It broke the Church's monopoly on scripture, fueled the Protestant Reformation, enabled the scientific revolution, and gave rise to the novel and the newspaper, fundamentally re-wiring the brains of individuals and the structure of societies. The "re-imagination" was not about faster scribes; it was about the possibility of a literate public and a world of mass communication. That is the scale of reimagination required today.

To make this practical, leaders must employ tools of "speculative design." This involves creating tangible artifacts from a potential future to make it feel real and to surface its hidden complexities. A government agency could, for example, hold a workshop to explore the "Personal Profile Digital-Twin" concept for healthcare. Instead of writing a policy paper, a team of designers, ethicists, doctors, and citizens would create mock-ups of the user interface. They might design the "consent dashboard" where a citizen grants access to their data. They might also produce a fictional news report from that future detailing how this system was used to deny someone insurance, or a short film about an elderly person whose Digital-Twin helps them live independently.

These artifacts are not predictions; they are provocations. They move the conversation from the abstract to the concrete, allowing for a far richer debate about the ethical and social implications of a proposed future before a single line of code is written.

UNLEAR to LEARN

This is the humble acknowledgment that our past successes and existing expertise are now potential liabilities.

We must have the humility to unlearn the ingrained habits, bureaucratic orthodoxies, and outdated assumptions that hold us back.

This unlearning is an active and painful process of intellectual and cultural demolition. It means identifying and dismantling the core tenets of the industrial-era bureaucracy: the sanctity of hierarchical decision-making, the fierce ownership of siloed information, the reliance on paper-based audit trails as the ultimate source of truth, and the deeply ingrained belief that risk is something to be eliminated rather than managed.

The barriers to this are deeply personal. For professionals who have built careers mastering a certain set of rules, unlearning can feel like a rejection of their identity and expertise. This "identity foreclosure" is a powerful force for inertia. Furthermore, the "sunk cost fallacy" pervades public sector IT; having spent billions on a legacy system, it feels impossible to abandon it, even when it is clear the system is a dead end.

Unlearning requires leaders to create psychological safety—to reward intelligent failure, to celebrate the decommissioning of old systems, and to create new career paths for those whose skills are becoming obsolete but whose institutional knowledge is invaluable. Without this, calls to "unlearn" will be met with fear and resistance.

PURPOSE DRIVEN

This is the anchor that prevents our transformation from becoming a purely technology-led exercise in novelty, a solution in search of a problem.

We must have the clarity to be driven by a purpose that serves the well-being of all our citizens, not just the interests of a few. Technology is a powerful tool, but it is not neutral. It is an accelerant. It amplifies the intent, values, and biases of its creators.

A focus on purpose ensures that we are constantly asking why we are building something, who it serves, what human values it promotes, and, crucially, who it might harm. This principle acts as a moral and ethical firewall against the seductive logic of technological solutionism.

These principles, while foundational for digital governance, apply with even greater force and urgency to the development of a Digital Society. We cannot simply layer a thin veneer of digital tools—a few government apps, a handful of e-services, a public Wi-Fi initiative—on top of an analog society and expect meaningful success. This approach is akin to putting a jet engine on a horse-drawn carriage.

The analogy is worth extending: the immense power of the engine does not just fail to make the carriage fly; it shatters its fundamental structure. The wooden wheels of social trust splinter under the speed of misinformation. The simple chassis of our legal frameworks buckles under the weight of global platforms that operate beyond the effective reach of national law. The reins of control, our governance models, snap as power shifts from sovereign states to non-state actors. The carriage will shatter. We must fundamentally rethink how people live, work, learn, and interact in a world of pervasive, hyper-digital connectivity. This is not about digitizing the edges of our society; it is about re-architecting its core.

Part II: Deconstructing "Purpose": Whose Purpose? Whose Power?

However, we must immediately confront a critical challenge to this framework, a point of intellectual friction that must be addressed head-on.

The principle to be "PURPOSE DRIVEN" begs the immediate and essential question: Whose purpose?.

In a pluralistic, democratic society, there is no single, monolithic purpose that can be dictated from on high. To suggest otherwise is to misunderstand the very nature of democracy, which is a system for managing conflict, not for achieving unity of thought. Citizens, communities, corporations, and civil society organizations harbor a multitude of competing, and often conflicting, interests and values.

The "purpose" of a technology platform designed to maximize shareholder value by capturing user attention is fundamentally different from the "purpose" of a public health system designed to promote equitable well-being. The "purpose" of a law enforcement agency seeking to expand surveillance capabilities is at odds with the "purpose" of a civil liberties group seeking to protect privacy.

Therefore, this principle cannot be interpreted as a call for a top-down declaration of a singular national purpose.

To do so would be to pave a road to authoritarianism, however well-intentioned. Rather, the principle must be refined. Being "purpose-driven" in the context of a Digital Society means creating a robust, transparent, and democratic framework within which these competing purposes can be articulated, debated, and negotiated. The purpose is not a destination decided by a few, but a continuous process of collective navigation guided by shared constitutional values of fairness, equity, and human dignity.

It is about designing a system—a political and social operating system—where the outcomes are not predetermined by the most powerful actor in the room.

An intelligent skeptic would push this point further, and they would be right to do so. They would argue that even the very idea of a "framework for negotiation" is dangerously naive, as it assumes a level playing field that simply does not exist in any modern society. This is not cynicism; it is a clear-eyed assessment of power.

The Skeptic's Analysis of Power

This skeptic's voice must be amplified, not dismissed.

They would argue that power in the digital age operates on several sophisticated levels.

First is the raw financial power of lobbying. Well-funded corporate lobbyists do not merely make donations; they provide armies of lawyers and public relations experts who draft ready-made legislation, fund academic studies that support their policy positions, and maintain a constant, influential presence in the halls of power, shaping the informational environment of lawmakers long before any public debate begins. Second is the power to define the problem itself. Powerful actors can frame the public conversation, ensuring that some issues (like "promoting innovation" or "national security") are perpetually at the forefront, while others (like algorithmic bias, data colonialism, or the mental health effects of social media) are marginalized or dismissed as secondary concerns.

The most effective form of power is to prevent your interests from ever becoming a subject of contention. Third is the weaponization of complexity and speed. The technical nature of digital policy and the sheer pace of technological change create an information asymmetry that benefits industry insiders. They can argue that regulation will "stifle innovation," a potent but often unsubstantiated claim that policymakers, lacking deep technical expertise, are ill-equipped to challenge.

Finally, the skeptic would point to the subtle but powerful influence of the "revolving door"—the constant flow of personnel between government regulatory bodies and the private sector corporations they are meant to oversee. A regulator who knows their next lucrative career move might be to a tech giant has a built-in, perhaps subconscious, incentive to maintain cordial relationships and avoid enacting policies that would alienate a future employer. This creates a culture of "soft capture" that is far more insidious than outright bribery.

Rebalancing the Scales of Power

Therefore, a truly "purpose-driven" approach must go beyond creating a neutral, passive space for debate; it must actively work to empower the powerless and rebalance the scales.

This is not about neutrality; it is about justice.

It is an affirmative action agenda for public discourse, requiring concrete, structural interventions:

- **Resourcing the Counter-Narrative**: It means providing stable, significant public funding for independent consumer advocacy groups and technology watchdogs. Imagine a "National Institute for **Digital Well-being**," funded by a small levy on the revenues of data-driven corporations. Its charter would mandate independence, and it would house divisions for Algorithmic Auditing, a Digital Literacy Curriculum Board, and a Social Cohesion Research Unit. Its findings would be public, providing lawmakers and citizens with an empirical counterweight to industry narratives.

- **Mandating Inclusive Governance through Co-Design:** It means ensuring that civil society organizations and representatives from marginalized communities have a formal, mandated seat at the policy-making table, not just as token consultants but as partners with real influence. This can be operationalized through mechanisms like **Citizens' Assemblies,** where a representative group of citizens, selected by lottery (sortition), are convened to deliberate on complex technology issues, supported by trained neutral facilitators and a balanced curriculum of evidence.

- **Forging New Legal Tools for Citizens:** It means creating new legal mechanisms that allow citizens to collectively challenge the decisions of both governments and corporations. The **"right to explanation"** for algorithmic decisions must be legally enforceable, coupled with a "right to human review." Furthermore, facilitating class-action lawsuits for data privacy violations aggregates the small harms suffered by millions into a claim large enough to act as a meaningful deterrent.

Without this proactive, structural rebalancing of power, any "negotiation" of purpose will simply be a performance, a public ritual that ratifies the pre-existing interests of the powerful. Justice, in the digital age, requires not just an open door, but a deliberate effort to help the less powerful walk through it, speak in their own voice, and be heard.

In short, the principle of being "Purpose Driven" can only be realized through a commitment to procedural justice, ensuring the system for defining our collective purpose is itself fair, inclusive, and balanced.

Part III: The Interwoven Pillars: Deconstructing the Model

The journey to becoming a Digital Nation, as I have conceptualized it, involves the transformation of three deeply interconnected pillars: **Digital Governance**, **Digital Economy**, and **Digital Society**.

My first book detailed how Digital Governance—the systems, laws, institutions, and culture of the state—is the foundational element.

A government that is not digitally native cannot hope to effectively regulate a complex digital economy or serve the needs of a dynamic digital society. This book explores the second pillar, Digital Society, which I define as "a social system where individuals engage, connect, and fulfill everyday needs through digital means".

A common and dangerous assumption is that a strong digital economy and an efficient digital governance will naturally, almost automatically, create a vibrant digital society.

This is a form of technological determinism, a belief that if we build the right platforms and achieve high rates of broadband penetration, a healthy society will simply emerge from the code. I challenge this assumption directly and forcefully.

A thriving Digital Society is not a byproduct; it is a prerequisite.

It is the fertile ground from which all else grows. Without a populace that is digitally literate and more important - competent, critically engaged, and fundamentally trusting of digital systems, even the most sophisticated government platforms will see low adoption, and the most innovative digital economies will fail to achieve inclusive growth.

You can build the most advanced digital highway in the world, but it is useless if citizens do not have the vehicles (devices and access), the skills (literacy and competency), or the trust (security and privacy) to travel on it.

However, the very model of three separate pillars, while useful for initial conceptual clarity, must be rigorously challenged.

Are they truly distinct, or is this an overly simplistic framework that masks the messy, overlapping, and often contradictory reality of their interactions?.

A critical analysis reveals that these pillars are not separate structures standing side-by-side. They are in a constant, dynamic, and often contentious relationship. The state, the market, and the community are locked in a complex dance, and the steps are being choreographed in real-time by technological innovation, corporate ambition, and geopolitical competition.

Society as Raw Material: The Logic of Data Extractivism

The "Digital Economy," for instance, is not a neutral, independent force.

It is dominated by a handful of global technology corporations whose business models are predicated on the capture and analysis of human attention, the harvesting of vast amounts of personal data, and the active shaping of social interactions to maximize profit.

In this more critical view, the Digital Society is not a prerequisite for the Digital Economy; it is the **raw material** for it.

This concept of "data extractivism" must be understood as a defining economic logic of our time. Just as the industrial economy extracted coal and iron ore from the earth, the digital economy extracts behavioral data from the substrate of human experience.

Our social interactions, our location history, our search queries, our emotional states inferred from our posts—all are mined, refined into predictive products, and sold in behavioral futures markets to advertisers and others.

This is a new form of colonialism, operating in the digital realm.

The great platform companies act as the new imperial powers, establishing outposts in nations around the world to extract a valuable local resource: the data of its citizenry. They define the "data territories" and lay claim to them through impenetrable terms of service. Local businesses and governments often become collaborators, dependent on the infrastructure and reach of these global platforms, in a way that benefits a small local elite but funnels the true value of the resource back to a foreign corporate metropole.

The struggle for data sovereignty, for community ownership of data, and for the rights of the "data subject" should thus be seen as a modern anti-colonial struggle.

Therefore, we must move beyond a simple, linear model and see these pillars as a constantly shifting, co-constitutive system. The relationship is a dynamic feedback loop.

The policies of Digital Governance (such as antitrust law) directly shape the structure of the Digital Economy. The business practices of the Digital Economy (such as targeted advertising) directly shape the norms of the Digital Society. And the values of the Digital Society (such as calls for greater privacy) can, in turn, put pressure on both government and industry to change. This is not a neat, orderly progression; it is a complex adaptive system.

The geopolitical dimension adds another layer of profound complexity, with the American (market-led), Chinese (state-led), European (rights-based), and Indian (public infrastructure) models competing to embed their values into the very protocols of the global internet.

This interconnectedness means that a failure in one pillar can cause a cascade of failures in the others, reinforcing the need for a holistic, not a siloed, approach to building a Digital Nation.

Part IV: The "Greenfield" Vision and the "Brownfield" Reality

To grasp the sheer scope of the transformation required, let's return to a powerful thought experiment: imagining a new country, "Terra Nova," built from scratch in the digital era.

With no legacy systems, no entrenched bureaucracies, and no outdated infrastructure to hold us back, how would we design its society?.

- **Community and Civic Life:** Civic life would be centered around secure, open-source digital forums designed to facilitate reasoned debate, not to maximize outrage. Political candidacy would be based not on fundraising, but on a publicly auditable digital portfolio of verifiable skills and contributions.
    - **The Skeptic's Critique:** Who designs the "reasonableness" algorithm? Such a system could easily enforce a bland, technocratic consensus, stamping out the passionate dissent that drives social progress.
- **Education:** Education would be a personalized, lifelong digital journey guided by an AI "learning companion," and credentials would be held in a dynamic "skills wallet," not a static degree.
    - **The Skeptic's Critique:** Who owns the data from this lifelong companion? This system could be used for predictive channeling of individuals into professions, reinforcing social stratification and creating a new divide of "algorithmic opportunity."
- **Healthcare:** A proactive health system would be centered around a citizen-controlled Personal Profile Digital-Twin, enabling predictive modeling and personalized treatments.

- **The Skeptic's Critique:** This is an ethical minefield, risking the creation of a "bio-social credit score" and a society of perpetual pre-patients, suffused with anxiety.

- **Justice and Law Enforcement:** Justice might be pursued through transparent systems, with predictive algorithms for social interventions and AI assistance for evidence review.
    - **The Skeptic's Critique:** This is a dystopian nightmare. Predictive policing trained on biased data becomes a high-tech mechanism for racial profiling, entrenching societal biases into the core of the justice system.

This "greenfield" thought experiment is not an argument for starting a new nation-state.

It is a call to action for leaders of existing nations to adopt the mindset of a digital native, to create a visionary "future state" that can serve as a North Star.

However, we must be brutally honest about its limitations.

Its greatest weakness is that no nation is a greenfield. The reality is a complex, layered "brownfield". We govern nations with centuries of history, ingrained cultural norms, aging infrastructure, and powerful vested interests. The practical strategy, therefore, cannot be one of demolition and reconstruction. It must be one of a master renovator: respecting the foundational structures of the old while artfully, strategically, and relentlessly weaving in the new. This means dealing with the messy realities of technical debt, institutional resistance, legal barriers, and cultural inertia.

The master renovator's toolkit is precise, including tools like **Policy Prototyping** in regulatory "sandboxes", **Strategic Procurement** to create markets for ethical tech, the active **Sunsetting of Laws**, and the creation of agile **Public-Private Skunkworks**.

The art of digital transformation, then, is this art of renovation: knowing what to preserve, what to demolish, and what to build anew, all within the complex reality of an existing structure.

Part V: The New Social Contract: From Implicit Agreement to Explicit Architecture

This profound shift from an analog to a Digital Society necessitates the forging of a new social contract.

The original social contract, as envisioned by enlightenment philosophers like Locke and Rousseau, was an implicit agreement to cooperate for social benefits, sacrificing some individual freedom for state protection. That contract was primarily concerned with protecting the physical body from violence and securing physical property from theft. Our world of global platforms and algorithmic mediation is fundamentally different. The threats are no longer just to our physical selves, but to our cognitive autonomy, our social cohesion, and our collective sense of reality.

Therefore, this new social contract cannot be an implicit understanding; it must be an explicit architecture. It must be embedded in the code of our platforms, the text of our laws, and the charters of our institutions. It is the battlefield where the competing interests of the State, the Corporation, and the Citizen will clash for the next century.

This requires a complete demolition of the current "notice and consent" paradigm, a legal fiction that fails at a fundamental psychological level due to "decision fatigue" and "bounded rationality."

A new, explicit social contract would be built on a foundation of citizen empowerment, manifest in three core architectural pillars:

1. **A Shift from Consent to Fiduciary Duty:** The cornerstone must be a shift to a legally enforceable fiduciary model, where platforms handling personal data have a duty to act in their users' best interests. This would make business models based on surveillance and behavioral manipulation legally untenable, forcing an alignment of corporate interests with user well-being.

2. **The Creation of Collective Bargaining through Data Trusts:** To address the profound power imbalance, the new contract must enable the creation of independent "data trusts"—new legal entities that collectively manage and bargain on behalf of citizens, acting as the data unions for the 21st-century information economy.

3. **A Constitutional Digital Bill of Rights:** The new social contract must be codified in our highest laws, establishing inalienable rights for the digital age, including: The Right to Algorithmic Transparency and Explanation, The Right to Human Review, The Right to Data Portability and Erasure, The Right to Freedom from Pervasive Surveillance, and The Right to Disconnect.

Without these robust, structural safeguards, the "New Social Contract" will simply be a new set of terms and conditions, written in even finer print, imposed by the powerful on the powerless.

The task ahead is not to predict the future, but to design it by embedding our highest values—dignity, equity, and liberty—into the digital architecture that will shape our lives for generations to come.

Chapter 2:

The Enablers and the Ecosystem of a Digital Society

A successful Digital Society does not materialize out of thin air. It is not the result of wishful thinking or grand pronouncements. It is built upon a foundation of robust, accessible, and secure infrastructure, and it is fueled by a digitally empowered and critically-minded citizenry.

These are the core enablers, the essential preconditions for transformation. Without them, even the most ambitious and well-intentioned plans for a digital future will fall short, creating a landscape of failed projects, underutilized platforms, and deepening social divides.

This chapter deconstructs the ecosystem of these enablers, moving beyond simplistic labels to explore the complex political, economic, and social realities that underpin them.

The concept of an ecosystem is critical here; these enablers are not a simple checklist of independent items. They are a deeply interconnected web where the health of each component depends entirely on the health of the others. A failure to provide equitable device access, for example, renders investments in digital literacy programs moot for a significant portion of the population. A lack of trusted digital identity undermines the security of the entire digital economy.

We will examine the physical and logical layers of infrastructure, the human capital of literacy, the crucial role of measurement, and the demographic forces that make this transformation inevitable, yet fraught with peril.

The "Roads and Bridges" of a Digital Society: A Deeper Look

Just as a 20th-century industrial economy relied on a network of roads, bridges, and power grids, a 21st-century Digital Society depends on a new kind of infrastructure. This digital foundation is the lifeblood of the nation, the circulatory system through which information, commerce, and social interaction flow.

It is a multi-layered ecosystem, and each layer presents its own profound challenges of politics, economics, and power.

Layer 1: Devices and Access - The Political Economy of Hardware

The most basic entry point to the Digital Society is a physical device. We often speak of this in simple terms of ownership—the percentage of the population with a smartphone or a laptop. But this framing obscures a complex political and economic reality.

The affordability and availability of these devices are not simple market outcomes; they are shaped by global supply chains, intellectual property regimes, and national industrial policies.

For most nations, the hardware is imported, creating dependencies on a few manufacturing hubs, primarily in East Asia. This dependency is not merely economic; it is a profound strategic vulnerability. The COVID-19 pandemic starkly revealed the fragility of these just-in-time supply chains, as a disruption in one part of the world led to immediate device shortages and dramatic price spikes across the globe.

Beyond pandemics, this centralization creates geopolitical chokepoints. The world's supply of advanced semiconductors, the brains of all modern devices, is dangerously concentrated in a few locations, most notably Taiwan. A geopolitical crisis in that region could halt the production of everything from smartphones to medical equipment, demonstrating how a nation's digital future can be held hostage by faraway conflicts.

Furthermore, the dominance of two operating systems—Google's Android and Apple's iOS—creates a powerful duopoly that gives these corporations immense power. This is not a benign market structure; it is a form of private governance that operates on a global scale.

This power is wielded through their control of app stores, where they can levy a 15-30% commission on all transactions—a form of private tax extracted from local economies worldwide. It is wielded through their ability to unilaterally de-platform applications that compete with their own services or violate their often-opaque content policies, acting as judge, jury, and executioner in the digital marketplace.

This duopoly stifles innovation, forcing developers to operate in a permissioned environment where they must constantly cater to the rules and strategic interests of two gatekeeper corporations.

A truly strategic approach to the "device" layer requires moving beyond passive consumption and embracing a proactive industrial policy.

This involves creating policies that encourage local assembly or even manufacturing, not just for immediate economic benefit, but for the long-term goal of strategic autonomy. It means actively engaging with and promoting the global "right to repair" movement. This movement is not just about consumer rights; it is a direct challenge to the business model of planned obsolescence practiced by major manufacturers.

By using proprietary parts, software locks, and aggressive legal tactics, these companies make it difficult or impossible for consumers and independent technicians to repair devices.

A national right-to-repair law can foster a vibrant local ecosystem of repair businesses, extend the functional life of devices, reduce toxic e-waste, and, most importantly, make sustained digital access more affordable for everyone.

Finally, a strategic government must consider state-led initiatives to directly address affordability and access.

This could involve procuring and subsidizing low-cost, secure devices for students or low-income families. Such a program reframes the device not as a consumer luxury but as an essential tool for citizenship, as fundamental to 21st-century life as a textbook or a voter registration card.

Imagine a "public option" device: a secure, durable tablet running an open-source operating system, pre-loaded with essential public service and educational applications, and distributed through schools and social programs. Without sovereign capacity at this most basic layer, a nation is merely a tenant in its own digital home.

Layer 2: Digital Highways - The Geopolitics of Connectivity

If devices are the vehicles, then digital networks are the highways.

Here again, the challenge is far more complex than simply achieving a high percentage of broadband penetration.

The key issues that determine the character of a nation's digital future are **equity**, **quality**, and **control**.

The urban-rural divide is the most glaring equity challenge, a defining feature of the digital landscape in many developing nations where the reality is a tale of two countries. This is a predictable market failure. Private telecommunications companies, operating under a rational profit motive, will naturally invest their capital in densely populated urban areas where the return on investment is highest and fastest.

To expect otherwise is to misunderstand the fundamental logic of capital markets.

Addressing this deep-seated inequity requires a multi-pronged strategy that recognizes the limitations of the market. It means using policy levers to correct this failure, such as using the significant revenue generated from urban spectrum auctions to create universal service funds that directly subsidize the capital costs of rural infrastructure projects. It also requires a proactive exploration and support for alternative ownership models, such as community-owned networks, where local municipalities, non-profits, or citizen cooperatives build, own, and manage their own broadband infrastructure.

This approach not only keeps the economic benefits within the local community but also ensures that decisions about network upgrades, pricing, and service quality are tailored to local needs.

We must also embrace new technologies, but with a critical and clear-eyed perspective. The rise of low-Earth orbit (LEO) satellite constellations, such as SpaceX's Starlink, offers a tantalizing solution for connecting the most remote areas. However, this convenience introduces a new and profound set of geopolitical dependencies. A nation that becomes heavily reliant on a single, foreign-owned and operated satellite network for its entire rural connectivity is effectively ceding a degree of sovereign control over its critical national infrastructure.

It places the "off switch" for a significant part of its country's communication system in the hands of a foreign CEO and government, and routes its citizens' data through foreign systems.

The geopolitics of infrastructure are inescapable and represent a new "Great Game" for the 21st century. The competition between China's Digital Silk Road initiative and various Western-backed alternatives is a defining feature of our era. A decision to partner with a particular vendor is not just a technical or commercial choice; it is a profound geopolitical alignment with long-term consequences.

This decision can determine everything from the technical standards the country adopts (creating vendor lock-in), to its cybersecurity posture, to its diplomatic relationships for decades to come. It is the modern-day equivalent of choosing which empire will build your nation's railways.

Layer 3: Digital Identity - The Architecture of Trust and Control

A secure, trusted, and universally recognized digital identity is arguably the most critical and most contentious piece of infrastructure in the entire digital ecosystem.

It is the master key that unlocks meaningful participation in the digital world. However, the architectural choices made in designing such a foundational system have monumental and lasting implications for the relationship between the citizen and the state.

It is here that a society's deepest philosophical commitments about power, trust, and autonomy are cast into code. We can identify three broad models:

- **The Centralized Model: The All-Seeing State.** In this model, the government creates and manages a single, authoritative identity database. The prime example is **India's Aadhaar**, the world's largest biometric ID system. The stated benefits are enormous: reducing fraud, enabling financial inclusion, and streamlining access to services. However, the criticisms are equally profound. The creation of a single, massive database presents an irresistible target for cybercriminals and a terrifyingly powerful tool for state surveillance. The system has also led to exclusion, with reports of manual laborers with worn-down fingerprints being denied essential food rations because the system could not identify them. The core logic of the centralized model is one that prioritizes state efficiency and legibility, often at the expense of individual privacy and autonomy.

- **The Federated Model: A Constellation of Trust.** This model deliberately avoids a single central database. Instead, it allows a number of trusted identity providers—such as banks and government agencies—to issue digital credentials that are accepted across the system. **Estonia's system**, built on its revolutionary X-Road data exchange layer, is the leading global example. In the Estonian model, a citizen's data remains in its original, distributed locations, and the system simply passes secure, encrypted, and digitally signed messages back and forth. This model is generally considered more privacy-preserving and resilient. However, its success depends heavily on pre-existing conditions that may not be easily replicable elsewhere: a very high degree of social trust, a small and technically sophisticated population, and a long history of cross-sectoral collaboration.

- **The Self-Sovereign Identity (SSI) Model: The Empowered Individual.** This is the most radical, disruptive, and citizen-centric model. With SSI, the individual is placed in full and exclusive control of their digital identity. Using technologies like blockchain, individuals store their own "verifiable credentials" in a secure digital wallet on their own device. They can then present these credentials to any entity that needs to verify them, without needing to go through a central intermediary, and often in a privacy-preserving way (e.g., proving you are over 21 without revealing your date of birth). This model offers the greatest promise for privacy and user empowerment. However, it is also the least mature and introduces the daunting challenge of key recovery: if a user loses their private key, they could be permanently locked out of their own identity.

The choice between these models is a choice about where power should reside: with the state, with a federation of trusted institutions, or with the individual citizen.

A truly "purpose-driven" approach would likely involve a hybrid model, using a robust federated system for core government services while actively promoting the development of SSI for commercial and social interactions.

From Digital Literacy to Digital Competency: Cultivating Critical Consciousness

In a Digital Society, while **digital literacy** is often described as the new currency of citizenship, a more powerful and accurate goal is the cultivation of **digital competency**.

Literacy often implies the ability to read, understand, and critically evaluate information—an essential but fundamentally passive skill set. Competency, however, goes further; it is the confident, critical, and creative ability to *use* digital technologies to achieve goals, solve problems, communicate, and actively participate in civic and economic life.

It is the difference between being a critical consumer of digital content and being an empowered creator and agent in the digital world.

True digital citizenship requires this deeper competency, which is built on a range of sophisticated cognitive skills and foundational literacies.

It is a form of critical consciousness that allows individuals to navigate the complex and often polluted digital world with agency and discernment.

This includes:

- **Data Competency: The New Reading.** In a world awash with data, the ability to read, understand, create, and communicate with data as information is a fundamental survival skill. This means internalizing the basic principles of statistical reasoning: understanding that correlation is not causation, that sample sizes and methodologies matter profoundly, and that data can be visualized in misleading ways to support any conceivable conclusion. A competent citizen can not only spot a misleading chart but can also use basic data tools to analyze a public dataset and form their own conclusions.

- **Critical Media and Algorithmic Competency: Seeing the Matrix.** This is the modern evolution of media literacy: understanding and navigating the architectural biases of the algorithmic systems that now mediate our reality. A literate person understands their feed is personalized; a competent person knows how to take active steps to diversify their information diet, manage their privacy settings, and understand how their own data is being used to shape their experience. Citizens need to be taught that the information they see on social media or in search results is not an objective reflection of the world; it is a personalized, algorithmically curated feed designed with one primary goal: to maximize engagement.

- **Cybersecurity Competency and Collective Responsibility.** While individual responsibility is important, a critical perspective must challenge the prevailing narrative that places the entire burden of defense on the individual citizen. This is a subtle but pernicious form of systemic victim-blaming. A competent citizen knows how to use strong passwords and spot phishing scams, but they also understand that individual vigilance alone is insufficient. A truly robust Digital Society frames cybersecurity as a public good, designing systems that are safe and secure by default and holding corporations and institutions legally and financially liable for data breaches caused by their negligent security practices.

Many countries, particularly across Africa, are rightly prioritizing digital literacy programs, as highlighted by UNESCO.

However, as seen in country assessments for nations like Cameroon and Honduras, a significant portion of the population can be left behind without first addressing the high costs of access and ensuring that foundational digital skills are integrated into the core education curriculum from the earliest age.

This shift in focus from mere literacy to holistic competency is crucial. A truly robust Digital Society does not just train its citizens with the literacy to defend themselves in a dangerous and polluted information ecosystem; it empowers them with the competency to actively reshape that ecosystem for the better.

Measuring What Matters: The Politics of Indication

To truly understand our progress, we need to move beyond the narrow, technocratic metrics that currently dominate the field.

The UN's **E-Government Development Index (EGDI)**, while a useful starting point, primarily measures the supply side of digital government—the availability of online services. It tells us very little about the actual quality of those services, the equity of their distribution, or their real-world impact on people's lives.

To guide our transformation effectively, we need a new, more holistic toolkit of indicators that measure what truly matters.

I propose a new basket of indicators that would provide a much richer and more accurate picture of a nation's digital health:

- **Social Cohesion Index:** A sophisticated measure that analyzes massive datasets of public digital discourse to gauge the extent to which online platforms are being used for positive community-building versus fueling polarization and hate speech.
- **Digital Inclusion Rate:** This metric would track not just raw internet penetration, but how equitably access, skills, and, most importantly, outcomes are distributed across all demographic groups. The gender

gap in internet use, for example, remains a serious issue in countries like **Tanzania** and **Myanmar**, as reported by the GSMA, effectively locking half the population out of the benefits of the digital world.

- **Digital Services Adoption and Satisfaction Rate:** This moves beyond simply counting available e-services to measuring what percentage of the eligible population actually uses them and their satisfaction with the experience. The case of **Switzerland**, which consistently ranks highly on the supply-side EGDI but suffers from demonstrably low citizen satisfaction with its e-services, perfectly demonstrates this critical gap.

A thoughtful skeptic, however, would rightly object that what gets measured gets managed—and often, gamed.

This is a restatement of Goodhart's Law: "When a measure becomes a target, it ceases to be a good measure." To prevent governments from simply "teaching to the test," it is essential that these measurement frameworks be developed and managed by independent, multi-stakeholder bodies—comprising academics, civil society groups, private sector experts, and government representatives—with full transparency in their methodologies and raw data.

The "Digital Native" Generations: Catalyst or Complacent?

The shift to a Digital Society is not just a policy choice; it is a demographic inevitability.

This transformation is being driven, accelerated, and defined by the emergence of new generations who have never known a world without the internet. **Generation Z** (born roughly between 1997 and 2012) and **Generation Alpha** (born since 2013) are the primary catalysts for this change.

As the first true digital native populations, their baseline expectations for how the world should work are fundamentally and irrevocably different from those of their predecessors.

Their collective impatience with analog, bureaucratic, paper-based, and inefficient systems will be the single most powerful force compelling governments and legacy institutions to adapt or be left behind. This is not a matter of preference or convenience; for these generations, it is a matter of legitimacy.

A state that cannot interact with its citizens on the platforms and in the manner they expect will increasingly be seen as incompetent, out of touch, and fundamentally illegitimate.

However, we must rigorously challenge the utopian and often complacent narrative that "the kids will save us". Being a "digital native"—fluent in the use of TikTok and video games—is no defense against sophisticated state-sponsored disinformation campaigns and may even breed a dangerous complacency about foundational issues like data privacy and algorithmic bias.

The fish is the last to discover water. For digital natives, the personalized feeds and algorithmically mediated realities of the platform world feel "natural," and this very naturalness can lower their critical guard, making them perhaps more susceptible to certain forms of manipulation and commercial exploitation.

The profound challenge for educators and policymakers is to ensure that the intuitive fluency these generations have with the how of digital tools is matched by a deep and critical understanding of the why and the by whom.

Without this critical consciousness, the digital natives risk becoming the most sophisticated and compliant consumers in history, navigating their gilded digital cages with dazzling technical skill but with little true agency or control over their own lives and choices.

Part II:

Core Elements of a Reimagined Digital Society

Chapter 3:
The Digital Town Square: Reimagining Community and Civic Life

The metaphor of the "Digital Town Square" is one of the most enduring and powerful images in the discourse surrounding the Digital Society.

It evokes a romantic, almost nostalgic picture of a vibrant public commons where citizens gather as equals to debate the issues of the day.

It is a beautiful image. It is also profoundly misleading.

To speak of reimagining community and civic life in the digital age requires us to first perform a radical deconstruction of this faulty metaphor and analyze these spaces for what they truly are: privately-owned, commercially-driven, and algorithmically-engineered environments designed not for civic discourse, but for the maximization of user engagement for profit. The architecture of these spaces is not neutral; it is a powerful and often invisible force that shapes our discourse and influences our behavior.

Today's primary "town squares" are not public parks; they are shopping malls.

The Architecture of the Mall: From Public Forum to Persuasive Space

A traditional town square is public land.

Its rules are, in theory, set by a democratic process.

A shopping mall, conversely, is private property. Its rules, its "terms of service," are set unilaterally by its corporate owner to facilitate commerce. You are welcome, but only as a potential consumer. Certain forms of speech, like organized protests, are typically forbidden. The very architecture is meticulously engineered to encourage specific behaviors, namely Browse and buying.

The architecture of the digital square is no different, only far more sophisticated and psychologically invasive. It is an architecture of behavioral modification. Features like the "Like" button and the "infinite scroll" are deliberate design choices that foster a state of continuous, passive consumption.

The notification systems are engineered to be psychologically compelling, creating a system of "intermittent variable rewards"—much like a slot machine—that keeps us compulsively checking our devices. Most importantly, the recommendation algorithm is the invisible, unaccountable hand that curates our individual realities.

This atomizes the public, destroying the possibility of a shared "common knowledge" base from which to begin a debate. This is not a civic architecture; it is a commercial one, a Foucauldian Panopticon where the knowledge of being constantly watched by an algorithm leads users to internalize the logic of the system, performing a version of themselves they believe will be rewarded.

The Promise and Pitfalls of E-Participation

Within this challenging commercialized landscape, the formal effort by governments to engage with citizens online, known as E-participation, represents a crucial attempt to carve out a dedicated civic space.

This ranges from **e-information** (making data accessible), to **e-consultation** (inviting public feedback), to **e-decision-making** (involving citizens in policy, such as participatory budgeting platforms in cities like Paris or Lisbon). When it works, it holds the promise of a more responsive and participatory democracy.

The Pioneers: Models of Digital Governance

Global leaders offer compelling models. **Estonia** is renowned for its comprehensive e-governance ecosystem, including secure i-voting and the "once-only" principle, a legal mandate ensuring citizens need only provide a piece of personal information to the state once. **Denmark** consistently ranks as one of the best for its integrated and relentlessly user-centric e-services. **South Korea** has cultivated a highly engaged citizenry that actively uses digital platforms to petition for policy changes and hold officials accountable.

The Dark Side of Efficiency: A Critique of the Leaders

However, a critical analysis must also examine the potential downsides. Estonia's all-in approach, while impressively efficient, creates a single, nation-scale point of failure, making it hyper-vulnerable to a catastrophic cyberattack.

Furthermore, the relentless focus on digital-first can create a "cold" efficiency, potentially alienating citizens who are less digitally savvy. In South Korea, the same digital fervor that fuels democratic accountability can also manifest as intense online pressure campaigns and cyber-bullying directed at public figures, blurring the line between legitimate criticism and toxic harassment.

The Causality Dilemma: Trust as a Precondition

A critical question hangs over these success stories: one of causality. Does high e-participation create good governance and a trusting society, or does a pre-existing culture of high social trust and effective governance enable widespread e-participation?

The evidence from a global comparison strongly points to the latter. Technology is an accelerator, not a cause. It amplifies existing social dynamics.

This is starkly illustrated by the "laggards." A high-income nation like **San Marino** struggles with low e-participation rates not because of a lack of resources, but because of deeper issues of political culture. More dramatically, a wealthy nation like **Kuwait** has seen a massive decline in its e-participation score, a clear signal that simply investing in technology without addressing underlying governance challenges is a recipe for failure.

Crisis as a Catalyst: The Case of Ukraine

Crisis can often be a powerful, if brutal, catalyst for change.

The recent case of **Ukraine** is a remarkable testament to this phenomenon.

Forged in the crucible of invasion, its "Diia" app has become a global exemplar of e-participation and national resilience.

It has become a genuine lifeline for millions, used to receive financial aid, report enemy troop movements, and maintain a tangible connection to their state in the face of an existential threat. However, the wartime unity that made Diia so effective is a unique condition.

The intense "state-citizen fusion" born of a shared struggle created a level of trust that is rarely seen in normal political life. The critical challenge is how to foster and maintain that sense of shared purpose and trust in times of peace.

The Peril of the Corporate-Owned Square

While government platforms are important, the dominant arenas of daily interaction are the massive social media platforms.

Their perils are not accidental bugs; they are the logical, predictable, and profitable outcomes of their fundamental business model. This model can be broken down into a simple, relentless logic: the goal is to maximize user time-on-platform.

The method is the constant collection of vast amounts of behavioral data. The product sold is access to the user's attention and the ability to influence their behavior. Within this model, anything that increases engagement is, by definition, good for business.

The consequences of this logic are severe and systemic.

- **Consequence 1: Misinformation and Disinformation: The Architecture of Falsehood**

  The algorithms are designed to promote content that elicits strong emotional reactions. Unfortunately, outrage, fear, and sensationalism are powerful emotions. As a direct result, these platforms have become super-spreaders of "fake news" and conspiracy theories. This has given rise to sophisticated tactics like the "Firehose of Falsehood," a disinformation model where the goal is not to convince people of a specific lie, but to overwhelm them with so many contradictions that they begin to distrust all sources of information, cultivating a pervasive and corrosive cynicism.

- **Consequence 2: Digital Silos and Echo Chambers: The Architecture of Polarization**

  Personalization techniques create insulated "echo chambers" where individuals are only exposed to information that confirms their existing beliefs. This process arguably has a neurological impact, hijacking our evolutionary wiring for in-group loyalty. By constantly feeding us information that affirms our "tribe" and demonizes the "other," these platforms can make political differences feel less like policy disagreements and more like existential battles, starving society of empathy.

- **Consequence 3: Cybercrime and Insecurity: The Architecture of Vulnerability**

  The centralized nature of these platforms and the vast troves of personal data they collect makes them prime targets for criminals seeking to commit identity theft and financial fraud. Furthermore, the general climate of insecurity and the normalization of digital attacks, including ransomware attacks on critical infrastructure like hospitals and schools, can undermine the very credibility and trustworthiness of a digital state.

The State's Dilemma: Security, Trust, and Control

The state's role in this new landscape is fraught with contradiction. It faces both unprecedented challenges to its security and unprecedented temptations to expand its power.

The Mandate for Protection

On one hand, the state has a fundamental responsibility to protect its citizens and institutions from digital threats.

The statistic that a staggering 12% of all cybercrimes in Africa are directed at government agencies is deeply alarming. It underscores the acute vulnerability of nascent digital states. Governments must therefore invest heavily in robust cybersecurity measures, including building national Computer Emergency Response Teams (CERTs) and fostering a domestic cybersecurity industry.

The Temptation of Control and the Rise of the Digital Leviathan

On the other hand, the very tools of e-government and digital security can be repurposed for surveillance and social control.

The case of **Myanmar** provides a stark reminder of this danger. Following the military coup, the junta has actively weaponized digital tools, using systems like a national census and an e-ID project to strengthen state surveillance and track dissidents. This is a textbook example of "function creep," where a system designed for one purpose is later used for another, far more sinister one.

This danger is evolving.

States are moving beyond reactive surveillance to embrace predictive governance.

By ingesting massive datasets, states can build analytical models to "predict" who might become a dissident or a criminal. This leads to the specter of "pre-crime" systems, which punish individuals for who they might be, fundamentally reversing the presumption of innocence.

Guarding the Guards: The Imperative of Democratic Oversight

A digital society is only as good as the values that guide it and the legal and institutional constraints that bind its use of power.

The technology itself is agnostic; the difference lies not in the code, but in the governance that surrounds the code.

This requires building a comprehensive framework of democratic accountability, including: **Strong, independent Data Protection Authorities (DPAs)** with budgetary autonomy and real enforcement power; **dedicated parliamentary oversight committees** with independent technical expertise; a **vibrant and legally protected civil society** to act as public watchdogs; and **constitutional or charter-level rights** that enshrine digital privacy and freedom from pervasive surveillance.

Ultimately, the great challenge is to build a Digital Society that reaps the benefits of technology without succumbing to its temptations of control.

Chapter 4:

Digital Education: From Schools to Lifelong Learning

The rapid and stunning ascent of generative artificial intelligence has thrust the global education sector into a new period of profound uncertainty and immense opportunity.

The assertion that we must now prepare citizens not just for a digital world, but for a "Generative AI Native" world, is both timely and unavoidable. However, to focus solely on the latest technological trend is to risk a dangerously narrow view of education's purpose. The true transformation required is deeper.

It lies in shifting the core focus of our educational systems from teaching what to know to teaching how to think.

A thoughtful skeptic would rightly argue that this call is as old as education itself, and that the real, enduring challenge is to cultivate intellectual virtues—curiosity, skepticism, intellectual humility—that are fundamentally technology-agnostic.

The tool will always change; the quality of the mind using it is what truly matters.

Part 1: The New Educational Philosophy: From Knowing to Thinking

The industrial-era model of education was designed to produce a workforce for an industrial economy, prioritizing standardization and the memorization of a stable body of knowledge. That world no longer exists.

The Obsolescence of 'What': The Economics of Instant Answers

The economic logic underpinning the old model has evaporated.

Generative AI has now driven the marginal cost of retrieving and summarizing factual information to effectively zero.

Any job or profession whose primary value is based on the recall and synthesis of existing information is now at existential risk of automation. Therefore, the shift in education from teaching "what to know" is not a high-minded philosophical preference; it is an urgent economic imperative.

Continuing to focus on rote memorization is a profound disservice to young people, preparing them for jobs that will no longer exist.

Deconstructing 'How to Think': A Modern Trivium for the Digital Age

What does it mean to teach "how to think" in practice?

We can give it structure by conceptualizing a modern version of the classical Trivium, focusing on four interdependent competencies:

1. **Critical Thinking and Intellectual Humility:** This is the bedrock skill. It is the ability to analyze information, identify biases, evaluate evidence, and construct a reasoned argument. It means teaching practical methods for source evaluation, such as the S.I.F.T. method (Stop; Investigate the source; Find better coverage; Trace claims). More deeply, it means cultivating the intellectual virtue of humility—the ability to recognize the limits of one's own knowledge.

2. **Creativity and Synthesis:** As AI becomes proficient at analytical tasks, the premium on human creativity will soar. This is not merely about artistic expression; it is about the ability to connect disparate ideas to solve complex, unstructured problems. Educational systems must be redesigned to foster this through project-based learning that encourages experimentation and

tolerates failure.

3. **Collaboration and Digital Communication:** Complex global challenges require collaboration on a massive scale. Education must intentionally teach the skills of effective teamwork, particularly in digital environments. This includes learning how to manage conflict, build consensus in virtual teams, and navigate cross-cultural communication.

4. **Ethical Reasoning:** As technology gives humanity increasingly god-like powers, the ability to ask "Should we?" becomes infinitely more important than "Can we?". An education system that produces brilliant technologists who are ethically illiterate is creating a profound societal danger. This requires engaging with deep ethical frameworks—utilitarian, deontological, and virtue ethics—to give students the tools to analyze ethical dilemmas from multiple perspectives.

The Skeptic's Rebuttal: The Enduring Value of Core Knowledge

The skeptic would argue forcefully that this focus on abstract "skills" at the expense of concrete "knowledge" is a grave error.

They would contend that you cannot think critically about a subject you know nothing about. This argument is strongly rooted in the work of theorists like E.D. Hirsch Jr., who championed the concept of "cultural literacy." Hirsch argued that effective communication and a cohesive society depend on a shared body of background knowledge.

Without this common vocabulary of historical events, literary references, and scientific concepts, citizens lose the ability to understand allusions in public discourse. The skeptic's argument is not that skills are unimportant, but that deep, well-organized domain knowledge is the *prerequisite* for their effective application.

The challenge, therefore, is not to choose between "what to know" and "how to think," but to design a new educational model that does both.

Part 2: The Global Laboratory: Models and Imperatives

The traditional industrial-era model of education is no longer sufficient. Nations around the world are engaged in a great global experiment to reimagine the classroom, offering compelling, though diverse, models for what is possible.

Case Study 1: Singapore and the "Strategic State" Model

Singapore's Smart Nation Initiative represents a comprehensive, top-down strategy that deeply integrates technology into its world-class education system. The Singaporean model is explicitly and unapologetically aligned with its national economic strategy, with a strong emphasis on STEM fields. This is complemented by the nation's SkillsFuture program, a national movement for continuous lifelong learning. However, a critical perspective must ask about the potential downsides. The intense focus on economic competitiveness is a key driver of the national culture known as "Kiasu," a deep-seated fear of losing out, which contributes to extremely high levels of stress and anxiety among young people.

Case Study 2: Finland and the "Humanist" Model

In stark contrast, **Finland's** Digital Compass represents a more human-centric and trust-based model. Finland's strategy is built upon its long-standing tradition of teacher autonomy and a pedagogical focus on inquiry-based learning and holistic student well-being. However, no model is a permanent panacea. In recent years, Finland has seen a notable decline in its PISA scores, sparking a national debate. Experts have pointed to several factors, including the distracting influence of smartphones on student concentration and challenges in supporting an increasingly diverse student population. This serves as a crucial reminder that even the most successful educational models must constantly adapt.

Case Study 3: Syria and the "Innovation from Constraint" Model

Perhaps more inspiring are the creative solutions emerging from environments of extreme constraint. The example of the **Syrian Ministry of Education**, facing the devastation of civil war, is a powerful case in point. Facing an inability to bring teachers together for traditional professional development, the Ministry has begun using 3D virtual reality to create immersive, interactive training modules that can be distributed digitally. This proves that groundbreaking innovation is not the exclusive domain of wealthy nations. Often, it is the absence of resources that forces a laser-like focus on the most pressing problem, leading to more robust and contextually appropriate solutions.

The Skills Gap vs. The Wisdom Deficit: An Existential Debate

The global demand for **ICT specialists** is dramatically outpacing supply. In Europe, countries such as **Belgium** and **Czechia** face a chronic shortage of ICT graduates. For a country like **Nigeria**, with its immense, youthful population, this skills gap represents a "demographic dividend"—a tremendous opportunity to become a global hub for tech talent. However, a myopic focus on producing coders and data scientists is a grave strategic mistake. A successful Digital Society needs more than just a technically proficient workforce; it needs a digitally literate citizenry. A society of brilliant engineers who have never studied ethics, history, or philosophy is a dangerous society. An overemphasis on STEM at the expense of the humanities does not truly solve a skills gap; it creates a different, and perhaps more dangerous, deficit—a deficit of wisdom, context, and critical perspective that leaves a society vulnerable to its own technological power.

Part 3: The Great Divider: The Challenge of Digital Equity

For all its promise, educational technology also presents one of the most significant threats to an inclusive Digital Society: the risk of deepening and amplifying existing inequalities. If not designed and implemented with a conscious, relentless focus on equity, technology in the classroom can act as a "threat multiplier" for existing social and economic disparities.

The Multi-Layered Digital Divide

The "digital divide" in education is a complex, multi-layered problem:

- **The Access Divide:** This is the most basic gap, concerning physical access to devices and reliable internet. In countries like **Nepal**, outdated curricula combined with a lack of trained teachers and infrastructure limit the opportunities for millions of young people, creating a geographic and economic lottery for digital opportunity.

- **The Skills Divide:** This is the gap between those taught to use technology as passive consumers and those taught to use it as active creators. This skills gap often maps onto existing socioeconomic divides, with students in affluent schools receiving a richer digital education.

- **The Opportunity Divide:** This third layer is the gap in the social capital and professional networks needed to translate digital skills into economic success. A student from an affluent background may have access to family connections and internship opportunities that an equally skilled student from a marginalized community may lack.

This multi-layered divide actively perpetuates inequality, creating a vicious cycle and the grim prospect of a durable, two-tiered society.

Technology as a Threat Multiplier

When technology is introduced into an already unequal system, it almost inevitably amplifies those inequalities.

This is especially true for students with disabilities.

A poorly designed educational technology platform can be a massive barrier to learning. A video lecture without captions excludes deaf students.

A drag-and-drop interface can be unusable for a student with a motor disability.

Most insidiously, technology can create the "data divide." As education becomes more data-driven, the high-quality data generated by students in affluent schools will be used to train and refine the most advanced AI-driven learning tools. These superior tools will then be sold back to the affluent schools that can afford them, creating a feedback loop where the tools for the privileged get exponentially better.

The promise of personalized learning can easily curdle into a grim reality of personalized inequality.

Designing for Equity: From Threat Multiplier to Opportunity Engine

The dystopian outcome of a technologically-driven, two-tier society is not inevitable. It is a choice. We can choose to design and implement educational technology with equity as a core, non-negotiable design principle. This requires a proactive framework for action:

1. **Mandate Universal Design for Learning (UDL):** Governments must use their procurement power to mandate that all educational software and hardware purchased for public schools adhere to the principles of Universal Design for Learning, designing tools that are flexible and accessible from the outset.

2. **Establish Public Ownership of Educational Data:** The vast datasets generated by students in public school systems should be treated as a public good, not a private resource to be exploited by ed-tech vendors. This would mean establishing secure, anonymized public data trusts to train open-source, publicly-owned AI learning tools.

3. **Invest in Teachers, Not Just Technology:** The single most important investment for ensuring equitable outcomes is in the continuous, high-quality professional development of teachers. However, this commitment faces significant political and financial headwinds, including the political temptation to spend money on visible things

(like tablets) rather than on the less visible, long-term investment in teacher training. Overcoming this requires a political leadership that understands that an empowered, well-supported teacher is the most effective tool for equity that has ever been invented.

Ultimately, the challenge of digital education is a challenge of societal vision.

Will we allow technology to become a wedge that drives our societies further apart, or will we harness its power to build a more equitable, more creative, and more thoughtful generation of citizens?

The choice is ours.

Chapter 5:

Digital Health and Social Services: The Human-Centric Approach

Of all the domains ripe for digital transformation, the promise of a reimagined health and social services sector is perhaps the most profound and the most personal.

The potential to move from a reactive, sickness-based healthcare system to a proactive, wellness-focused model is a revolutionary goal. Similarly, the ability to deliver social support with dignity and precision can transform the social safety net. In navigating this high-stakes transformation, the guiding principle must be a relentless focus on the human-centric approach.

This chapter will explore both the transformative promise and the profound perils of this new frontier, first in the realm of health and then in social services, before concluding with a framework for ethical governance.

Part 1: The E-Health Revolution: Promise and Peril

The 20th-century model of healthcare was an architecture of reaction, with a "fee-for-service" economic model that rewarded activity rather than outcomes.

The 21st-century vision is to invert this model, creating an architecture of proactive wellness that is pervasive, personalized, predictive, and participatory.

The Architecture of Proactive Wellness: The Digital-Twin Vision

My vision for a transformed health system culminates in a world where all of an individual's personal health data is contained in a secure, private, and citizen-controlled **Personal Profile Digital-Twin**. This is a dynamic, lifelong health companion.

Its theoretical components include:

- **The Genomic Layer:** An individual's unique genetic code, providing insights into inherited predispositions and sensitivities.
- **The Clinical Layer:** The complete history of an individual's interactions with the formal healthcare system (EHRs). A successful Digital-Twin requires the universal adoption of open standards like HL7 FHIR (Fast Healthcare Interoperability Resources) to allow this data to flow seamlessly between providers.
- **The Real-World Behavioral Layer:** Dynamic, constantly updating data from an individual's daily life, captured from wearable devices, self-reported logs, and environmental sensors.
- **The Predictive Engine:** The AI-powered brain that continuously analyzes data from all layers to identify patterns, model disease risk, and simulate the effects of potential treatments.

Global Pioneers: Glimpses of the Future

Pioneering models around the world already demonstrate the potential of this trajectory.

Saudi Arabia's Seha Virtual Hospital is a stunning example, a "hospital without walls" that connects over 170 hospitals, allowing top specialists to conduct remote consultations and even participate in remote heart surgeries, democratizing access to elite expertise. Other nations offer glimpses into different facets.

Estonia's nationwide e-Health Record system is a masterclass in interoperability and citizen empowerment.

In **Rwanda**, the partnership with Zipline showcases innovation in logistics, using autonomous drones to deliver blood products and vaccines to remote health clinics.

In the **United Kingdom**, the NHS App is a citizen-facing portal designed to be the "digital front door" to the health system.

The Perils of the Digital Panopticon: Deconstructing the Double-Edged Sword

However, the concept of the Digital-Twin is a double-edged sword.

The very features that make it so powerful also create a level of risk that is almost incomprehensible, containing the seeds of both a healthcare utopia and a dystopian surveillance society.

Cybersecurity as an Existential Threat

The Digital-Twin would be a target of immense value for cybercriminals and a tool of terrifying potential for authoritarian states.

Massive data leaks from government health systems, such as the breaches that exposed the personal information of millions of citizens in **India** and **Thailand**, fatally erode public trust. The threats are diverse. State-sponsored espionage, insider threats, and the rise of ransomware are all major concerns. The 2021 ransomware attack on Ireland's Health Service Executive (HSE) by a criminal gang crippled the nation's health system for weeks, demonstrating that a digital health system's dependency is its greatest vulnerability.

The Rise of the 'Biological Underclass': Algorithmic Discrimination

Beyond external attack, the Digital-Twin could become a powerful tool for a new, insidious kind of discrimination, creating a new "biological underclass," defined and limited by their data.

This goes beyond simple discrimination to a form of "biopower," a concept described by philosopher Michel Foucault, where states exert control over populations by managing their biological life.

This risk manifests in several domains:

- **Insurance and Financial Services:** Predictive data could be used to deny coverage or charge prohibitive premiums to those with pre-existing genetic conditions, undermining the very principle of pooled, social risk.
- **Employment:** The danger of "we-hiring"—the practice of hiring for wellness—is immense. Employers could use it to screen out applicants deemed to be at higher risk for future health problems. The specific risk surrounding mental health data is particularly acute.
- **Proxy Discrimination:** The danger is made more complex by "proxy discrimination." An algorithm may be legally forbidden from using a protected characteristic like race, but it can use thousands of other data points—like zip code or purchasing history—that are highly correlated with race to achieve the same discriminatory outcome.

The Ethics of Nudging, Autonomy, and the Quantified Self

Even in a perfectly secure system, a deeper ethical dilemma emerges around personal autonomy.

At what point does a "health companion" that constantly "nudges" you to exercise or eat better become a tool of coercion?

We can analyze this through the lens of **Principlism**, a dominant framework in bioethics (autonomy, beneficence, non-maleficence, justice). A digital nudge may satisfy beneficence (it aims to do good) but can directly conflict with **autonomy**, the right of an individual to make their own informed, uncoerced decisions.

This "libertarian paternalism" risks creating a society of anxious individuals, constantly monitoring their "quantified self" and feeling guilty for any deviation from an algorithmically-defined optimum.

Part 2: Re-engineering the Social Safety Net

Digital technologies also hold the power to re-engineer social services, making them more efficient, transparent, and responsive to human need.

For too long, social assistance has been plagued by bureaucracy, high administrative costs, and debilitating delays.

The Promise of Precision and Dignity

Innovative programs have demonstrated what is possible. During the COVID-19 pandemic, **Togo's** NOVISSI Program used a combination of AI-enabled analysis of mobile phone metadata and satellite imagery to rapidly target the most vulnerable informal workers for financial aid.

The success of this model relied heavily on academic partnerships and rigorous "ground-truthing," where researchers worked with communities to verify that the algorithmic proxies for poverty were accurate.

Similarly, in **Haiti**, a World Bank-funded program successfully used digital cash transfers to deliver assistance to vulnerable families, which not only provided a critical lifeline but also dramatically increased digital financial adoption.

Beyond agile targeting, digital systems can fundamentally reshape the experience of receiving aid, restoring dignity by reducing the "time tax" of bureaucracy and empowering recipients with choice through direct cash transfers.

The Perils of the Algorithmic Welfare State

The tools themselves are morally neutral.

The same technologies that promise a more efficient safety net can also create a more invasive, biased, and punitive system of social control.

- **The Surveillance Dilemma: From Social Support to Social Control.** The data-driven nature of these systems creates an inherent surveillance dilemma. The same AI that identifies a vulnerable worker in Togo could just as easily be used by an authoritarian regime to identify a political protestor. The "function creep" potential is immense: a system designed to verify eligibility for welfare can be repurposed to monitor the behavior of recipients or restrict how they can spend their benefits.

- **Automating Inequality: The Bias in the Machine.** A further danger lies in the rise of automated fraud-detection algorithms. These systems are often trained on biased historical data, leading them to reproduce and amplify existing societal prejudices. This creates a "digital poorhouse," an automated system that subjects the poor to a relentless cycle of suspicion. This can be exacerbated by the "Matthew Effect" ("the rich get richer"), where automated systems, being more easily navigated by the digitally literate, can inadvertently channel more benefits to those who need them least.

- **The Exclusion Problem: The Unidentifiable and the Unconnected.** The push towards digital-first social services creates a significant risk of exclusion for those who cannot easily navigate the new system, such as individuals experiencing homelessness, refugees, and the elderly. A particularly acute challenge arises for survivors of domestic violence. A digital-first system can be actively dangerous for someone trying to escape an abuser who may control their phone and finances. A mandatory digital-first system that does not provide robust and respectful analog alternatives is a system of exclusion.

Part 3: Governance: The Human-Centric Imperative

The journey toward a digital future for health and social services is paved with both promise and peril. The difference between a utopian outcome and a dystopian one is not technology; it is governance. The guiding principle must be a relentless focus on the human-centric approach.

This requires a non-negotiable foundation of ethical governance, including several key pillars:

1. **Fierce, Independent Oversight:** Government agencies and private companies must be subject to oversight from independent, well-resourced bodies. This means creating Data Protection Authorities (DPAs) that are politically independent, possess deep technical expertise, and have the legal authority

to levy meaningful fines.

2. **Radical Transparency and Explainable AI (XAI):** The use of algorithms in high-stakes decisions must be transparent. The legal and ethical standard should be clear: if a system's decision-making process cannot be rendered in plain language to the person it affects, it should not be used.

3. **Clear Avenues for Appeal and Redress:** When an automated system makes an error, there must be a simple and accessible process for a human being to review and override that decision. Nations should consider establishing a specialized "Digital Services Ombudsman" to handle disputes.

4. **Ironclad Legal Frameworks and Digital Constitutionalism:** These systems must be governed by robust laws rooted in human rights. This includes comprehensive data protection laws and specific anti-discrimination laws. Ultimately, these frameworks should be seen as a form of "digital constitutionalism." We are living through a constitutional moment, where the choices we make now will define the nature of citizenship and the balance of power for the next century.

Efficiency must never come at the cost of human dignity or fundamental rights.

The ultimate goal is not just to build a faster system, but to build a fairer one.

This requires a conscious effort to embed our highest values—equity, privacy, autonomy, and dignity—into the very code and architecture of the digital systems that will shape the future of human life itself.

Part III:

The Way Forward: Cultivating a Purpose-Driven Digital Society

Chapter 6:

A Global View: Patterns, Challenges, and Opportunities

As we zoom out from the specific domains of education and healthcare to a global perspective, we see that the journey to a Digital Society is not a race with a single finish line.

It is a shared global experience, a complex tapestry woven from common threads of opportunity and challenge. While each nation's path is unique, shaped by its specific culture, economy, and political system, the underlying patterns are remarkably consistent.

The persistent digital divide, the evolving role of the state, and the growing imperative for international collaboration are universal themes.

This chapter synthesizes the core arguments of this book by examining these global patterns. It argues that the way forward requires a commitment to people-centric strategies that are globally informed but always locally adapted. Ultimately, we will find that building a successful Digital Society is less a technical challenge and more a political, economic, and moral one.

Part 1: The Persistent Divide: A Global Analysis of Digital Inequity

The most persistent and challenging pattern on a global scale is the digital divide.

Even in countries with high overall internet penetration rates, a significant and stubborn divide persists, most commonly between urban and rural populations. This is not a marginal issue; it is a central and structural barrier to creating a truly inclusive Digital Society.

National averages can be profoundly misleading, masking deep pockets of exclusion.

The Economics of Exclusion: Deconstructing the Market Failure

This divide is not a natural phenomenon; it is a predictable market failure.

The economics of telecommunications infrastructure are characterized by extremely high fixed costs and low marginal costs. This high degree of "capital intensity" makes the private telecoms sector behave much like the railroad or electricity utility companies of the 20th century, creating a natural monopoly or tight oligopoly. In densely populated urban areas, this model works for investors.

Rural areas present the opposite case, requiring vast infrastructure investment to reach a small number of customers. The result is a two-tiered system. In **Ghana**, for example, infrastructure is concentrated in Accra, creating two separate Ghanas. Similarly, in **Pakistan**, a lack of affordable broadband in rural areas prevents millions from participating in the digital economy.

Bridging this divide cannot be left to market forces.

It is a fundamental responsibility of the state, requiring purposeful public investment and creative regulatory policies that treat digital connectivity as an essential 21st-century utility, like electricity or clean water. This historical parallel is exact.

Just as programs like the Rural Electrification Act in the United States during the 1930s recognized that market forces would never connect the entire country, modern governments must adopt a similar mission-oriented approach to broadband.

Beyond Urban vs. Rural: The Intersecting Divides

A sophisticated analysis must recognize that the urban-rural divide is often a proxy for a more complex set of intersecting inequalities.

The digital divide is a multi-dimensional landscape of exclusion:

- **The Gender Divide:** In many parts of the world, gender is a primary determinant of digital access. Due to social norms, lower income levels, and disparities in education, women—particularly in rural areas of South Asia and Sub-Saharan Africa—are significantly less likely than men to own a mobile phone or use the internet.

- **The Generational Divide:** Older populations, even in affluent urban areas, can be profoundly digitally excluded. Many digital services are not designed with the needs of seniors in mind, which can lead to social isolation and disenfranchisement.

- **The Linguistic Divide:** The vast majority of content on the internet is concentrated in a handful of dominant languages, primarily English, Mandarin, and Spanish. This creates a significant barrier for speakers of minority or indigenous languages.

- **The Disability Divide:** In the rush to digitize, accessibility is often an afterthought. For people with disabilities, this can create new and insurmountable barriers. Websites and government portals that are not designed with screen reader compatibility in mind exclude the visually impaired. Complex interfaces can lock out individuals with motor disabilities.

Addressing the digital divide, therefore, requires a nuanced, intersectional approach that goes beyond simply laying cables.

It requires policies that specifically target women and girls, provide digital literacy training for seniors, promote local content in local languages, and mandate strict accessibility standards for all public-facing digital services.

Part 2: The Evolving State: From "Doer" to "Enabler" to... What?

A second universal pattern is the profound evolution required in the role of the state itself.

In the analog era, governments often saw their role as the primary "doer" or direct provider of all public services.

In the digital era, this model is no longer viable or desirable.

The complexity, pace, and cost of technological innovation mean that no government can or should do everything alone. The role of the state must evolve from being a direct provider to being an "enabler" of a broader digital ecosystem.

The "Enabler" State in Action: A Spectrum of Partnership

There are promising examples of this shift, illustrating a spectrum of partnership models:

- **The State as Convener: Paraguay's** InnovandoPY initiative is a prime example of the state acting as a convener and problem-broker, actively framing public challenges and seeking the best technology solutions from the private sector to solve them.

- **The State as Collaborator:** The robust public-private collaboration seen in countries like **Belgium** illustrates a deeper partnership model, particularly in building digital skills, where the government sets the national strategy and partners help execute it.

- **The State as a Platform:** A more advanced model is the "Government as a Platform" (GaaP) approach. Here, the government builds core, secure digital infrastructure—such as a national digital identity system and a digital payments gateway—and then makes it available to the private and non-profit sectors via open APIs. The UK's Gov.uk design system and India's "India Stack" are pioneering examples. This model requires a "thin" layer of government providing the core "operating system," which in turn enables a "thick" ecosystem of private and civic innovation.

The Skeptic's Corner: The Dangers of Abdication and Capture

A skeptic would rightly caution that this transition is fraught with significant risk. The language of "enabling" can easily become a euphemism for the abdication of public responsibility, for unchecked deregulation, and for the privatization of essential services without adequate oversight.

This raises two primary dangers:

- **The Risk of Abdication:** If a government simply outsources a critical public service to a private vendor without maintaining strong oversight, it risks catastrophic failure. If the vendor fails, citizens are left with little recourse, and the state may find it has lost the in-house capacity to fix the problem.

- **The Risk of Regulatory and Data Capture:** When government becomes heavily reliant on a few large private partners, there is a significant risk that these powerful corporations will use their deep expertise and resources to influence the "rules of the game" in their favor. A more modern version of this is "data capture," where a government becomes dependent on a single private partner, such as a major cloud provider, for the storage and management of its most sensitive citizen data. This creates a new form of national security vulnerability and a vendor lock-in that is extremely difficult to escape.

A truly successful enabler state does not simply step back.

It becomes a more sophisticated, active, and vigilant referee.

Shifting from a "doer" to an "enabler" does not require a weaker government; it requires a smarter, stronger, and more agile one, with new core competencies in sophisticated procurement, deep technical expertise, agile governance, and robust data stewardship.

Part 3: International Collaboration: From Cooperation to Contestation

No nation can complete the journey to a Digital Society in isolation.

The challenges are global, the supply chains are international, and the landscape of innovation is changing too quickly for any single country to master alone. International collaboration is not a luxury; it is a necessity.

The Power of Positive-Sum Collaboration

This collaboration is a powerful accelerator, allowing countries to share best practices and avoid reinventing the wheel.

- **Sharing Models and Standards: Estonia's** secure data exchange layer, the X-Road platform, is a prime example. Its success has not been confined to its borders; neighboring **Finland** has adopted it, and its principles have inspired systems in countries as diverse as **Peru** and the **Dominican Republic**. This open, cross-border knowledge sharing saves developing nations immense time and resources.

- **Building Coalitions of the Willing:** Networks like the Digital 9 (D9)—a collaborative group of leading digital nations—are dedicated to sharing best practices. Initiatives like GovStack aim to create common standards and reusable software "building blocks" for digital government services. These collaborations produce tangible outputs, such as shared open-source software repositories and joint research projects.

Collaboration as Counterbalance: The Geopolitics of Tech

Collaboration is also a necessary counterbalance to the immense structural power of global technology corporations.

Individually, most nations have little leverage. However, by working together to set global norms and standards for critical issues like data privacy and AI regulation, nations can create a more level playing field.

The "Brussels Effect" is a powerful illustration. The European Union's implementation of the GDPR has effectively set a de facto global standard for data privacy, as many global corporations find it simpler to adopt the EU's high standards across all their operations.

The Skeptic's Corner: The Arena of Great Power Competition

A clear-eyed skeptic, however, would argue that this optimistic vision masks a harsher reality.

International forums are often arenas for geopolitical competition. This has led to the growing fear of a "Splinternet"—the fracturing of the single, global internet into competing blocs, each with its own technical standards and ideology.

We can see at least three major blocs emerging: the market-driven US model, the state-centric Chinese model, and the regulatory, rights-based European model.

This competition plays out in crucial but obscure international standards bodies like the International Telecommunication Union (ITU), where nations lobby to have their domestic technical standards adopted globally.

A key battleground is the issue of "data localization," where countries pass laws mandating that their citizens' data must be stored on servers within their physical borders.

On one hand, these laws can be seen as a legitimate exercise of digital sovereignty. On the other, they can be seen as a form of digital protectionism and a tool for state surveillance.

For developing nations, this new great game presents a difficult set of choices. Aligning with one bloc may bring investment, but it may also mean importing a set of political values or creating long-term dependencies. The dream of a single, open, and global digital commons is under threat.

Chapter 7:

The Unfinished Work: A Call to Action

The path to a purposeful, just, and inclusive Digital Society is not a project with a defined endpoint.

It is not a summit to be conquered, after which we can rest.

It is, instead, a continuous journey of adaptation, learning, and course correction.

We are, and will always be, navigating a landscape that is being reshaped under our very feet by the relentless pace of technological change. Success in this endeavor requires not a rigid blueprint, but a moral compass and a durable set of guiding principles.

It requires a steadfast commitment to human-centric design, a culture of rigorous and honest self-assessment, and a courageous focus on truth over convenience.

The work is, and will always be, unfinished.

We stand at a moment in history as consequential as the dawn of the printing press or the start of the Industrial Revolution—a hinge point where the choices we make will have cascading effects for generations to come.

The technologies we are building are not merely tools; they are becoming the very substrate of our social, political, and economic lives. They are re-architecting what it means to be human, to be a community, to be a nation.

This final chapter, therefore, is not a conclusion in the traditional sense.

It is a call to action—for leaders who wield institutional power, for policymakers who write the rules, and for every citizen who has a stake in shaping our shared digital future.

It is an argument for a new kind of vigilance and a new kind of citizenship.

It is a framework for the difficult but essential work that lies ahead.

Part 1: The Individual Imperative: The Reimagined Citizen

The ultimate responsibility for building a healthy Digital Society lies not just with governments or corporations, but with each of us as individuals.

There are three clear reasons why this individual imperative has become so critical in our era.

First, the citizen is the fundamental building block and core ingredient of the state; a smarter, more engaged populace enables a smarter government, a smarter legislative, a smart judiciary, and a smart media.

Second, diminishing public and natural resources constrain the capacity of governments, requiring more active citizen participation to solve collective problems.

Third, the new and unique challenges of the digital age, from misinformation to cyber threats, are too complex and pervasive to be solved by top-down authority alone; they require the distributed power and intelligence of many.

The character of our digital world is the sum of billions of individual choices made every day.

While we must hold institutions accountable, we must also recognize our own agency and responsibility in this new landscape. To do so, we must cultivate and embrace a new conception of citizenship for the digital age.

This means moving beyond the passive role of a consumer of digital content or a user of government services, and becoming an active, engaged, and critical participant in our digital communities.

This is not a call for everyone to become a coder or a technologist. It is a call for a cognitive and ethical evolution in how we engage with the information ecosystem that surrounds us.

This reimagined citizen embodies three core virtues: the Critical Thinker, the Ethical Actor, and the Lifelong Learner.

The Critical Thinker: Waging a War on Certainty

The first and most fundamental role of the reimagined citizen is that of a **Critical Thinker**.

In an era of information scarcity, the primary intellectual virtue was knowledge—the possession of facts.

In our current era of information abundance, the primary intellectual virtue is discernment. The modern citizen is a triage nurse in an emergency room of information, constantly making high-stakes decisions about what to believe, what to dismiss, and what to question. To be a critical thinker in the 21st century means understanding that no information stream is neutral. It means recognizing that the algorithmically-curated feeds on our screens are not objective windows onto the world, but are personalized realities designed to maximize engagement, often by appealing to our most primal emotions of fear and outrage5.

It means actively fighting against the powerful psychological forces of confirmation bias (our tendency to seek out information that confirms our existing beliefs) and cognitive dissonance (the mental discomfort we feel when confronted with conflicting information).

This requires a practical toolkit for digital forensics.

It involves adopting methods like S.I.F.T. (Stop; Investigate the source; Find better coverage; Trace claims to the original context) not just for overtly suspicious news, but as a default mental habit for all information consumption.

It means cultivating the discipline to pause before sharing, to resist the dopamine hit of righteous indignation, and to become a node of friction and thoughtful deliberation in a system designed for frictionless emotional contagion.

Most profoundly, being a critical thinker means embracing intellectual humility.

In a digital world that rewards and amplifies absolute certainty, the quiet, humble admission of "I don't know" or "I might be wrong" is a radical act of civic courage.

The Ethical Digital Actor: From User to Steward

The second role is that of an **Ethical Digital Actor**.

This begins with a commitment to communicate online with the same respect and empathy we would ideally show in a face-to-face interaction. But it goes much deeper. It requires a shift in self-perception: from being a "user" of a platform to being a "steward" of the digital commons.

As a steward, the ethical actor understands that their online actions have consequences beyond their immediate view. They recognize that every "like," comment, and share is not just a personal expression, but is also a piece of training data that shapes the AI systems that govern the platform for everyone. Sharing an outrageous but unverified story, for example, not only misinforms one's own network but also teaches the algorithm that this type of content is engaging, making it more likely that similar content will be shown to others.

This stewardship model involves a proactive commitment to digital sanitation.

It means refusing to participate in the spread of hate speech or disinformation, not just by refraining from posting it, but by actively reporting it and, where possible, by offering reasoned counter-arguments.

It means protecting the privacy of others, thinking twice before sharing photos or personal information about someone else without their explicit consent. It means a commitment to de-escalation, choosing to step away from a toxic online argument rather than adding to the negativity.

It is the recognition that the health of our digital public square is a collective responsibility, built or broken by the sum of our individual actions.

The Lifelong Learner: Embracing Perpetual Beta

The third role is that of a **Lifelong Learner**.

The industrial-era model of education—where one learned a trade or profession in their youth that would last a lifetime—is obsolete.

In the digital age, the pace of technological change means that skills are not static; specific competencies will become outdated at an accelerating rate.

To remain relevant and economically secure, the reimagined citizen must embrace a state of "perpetual beta"—a mindset of continuous learning, adaptation, and reinvention. This is more than just periodically taking an online course. It is a fundamental shift in identity. It requires the psychological flexibility to "unlearn" old mental models and skills that are no longer effective, which is often more difficult than learning something new.

It means cultivating an insatiable curiosity and actively fighting against the information fatigue that can lead to complacency.

In practical terms, this involves building a Personal Learning Network (PLN)—a curated set of sources, experts, and communities that help one stay abreast of changes. It means embracing micro-credentials and alternative forms of certification to validate new skills.

It means adopting a project-based approach to one's own development, constantly seeking out new challenges and opportunities to apply new knowledge.

In a world of constant change, the most valuable asset is not what you know, but how quickly and effectively you can learn.

These three internal virtues, however, are meaningless unless they are translated into external action.

When a citizen cultivates the mind of a Critical Thinker, the conscience of an Ethical Actor, and the adaptability of a Lifelong Learner, they manifest these qualities in the public sphere through the concrete roles of a "Flag Raiser," a "Solution Provider," and a "Change Agent".

As a Flag Raiser, they use their critical eye to identify issues and bring them to the notice of public authorities.

As a Solution Provider, they leverage their knowledge and digital capabilities to help create sustainable solutions, either independently or in collaboration with the state.

And as a Change Agent, they play an active role as a stakeholder in the nation's progress, driving communities to bring about positive change.

It is this powerful combination of internal virtue and external action that truly defines the reimagined citizen.

The Skeptic's Intervention: The Limits of Individual Responsibility

A clear-eyed skeptic would argue, with considerable justification, that this vision of a "reimagined citizen" places far too much onus on the individual.

While individual responsibility is important, it is not a sufficient substitute for systemic change and corporate and state accountability.

To expect an individual, through sheer willpower and critical thinking, to single-handedly fight back against a multi-trillion dollar industry designed by teams of PhD-level behavioral scientists to capture their attention and manipulate their behavior is both unfair and unrealistic. It is akin to telling citizens living downstream from a polluting factory that the solution to the contaminated water is for them to simply become better at boiling and filtering it.

The real solution is to regulate the factory.

This individualistic framing can be a dangerous diversion, a way for powerful systems to evade their responsibilities.

The language of "personal responsibility" is often co-opted by those who benefit from the status quo. The primary problem is not a deficit of citizen virtue; it is a deficit of systemic integrity. We need to design better, safer, and more transparent systems; we cannot simply expect to educate our way out of the problems created by a flawed and extractive platform architecture.

This skeptical critique is not a dismissal of individual responsibility, but a necessary correction to its over-emphasis. The call for a "reimagined citizen" must be paired with an equally forceful, and arguably more important, call for reimagined platforms and reimagined regulation.

The empowered citizen can only truly exist and thrive within an empowering ecosystem.

Part 2: The Systemic Imperative: Reimagining Our Institutions

The reimagined citizen cannot be willed into existence in a vacuum.

They need an environment that supports and encourages critical thinking, ethical action, and lifelong learning.

This requires a fundamental reimagining of the most powerful institutions that shape our digital world: the Corporation and the State.

Reimagining the Corporation: Beyond Surveillance Capitalism

The core architectural problem of our current digital public square is that it is governed by the logic of surveillance capitalism.

The solution, therefore, requires a new architecture governed by a different logic. This does not mean destroying corporations, but it does mean forcing them to evolve beyond their current, harmful business models.

A reimagined digital platform would be built on three pillars: new business models, humane design, and a fiduciary duty of care.

- **New Business Models:** The dominance of the advertising model is not inevitable. We must create the regulatory space and consumer demand for alternatives. This includes subscription models (where users pay for a high-quality, ad-free experience), membership models (as seen in platforms like Substack or Patreon, which support creators directly), and public-private partnerships (where public funding supports the creation of non-commercial digital spaces). Another powerful model is the creation of data trusts, where users could pool their data and collectively bargain for how it is used, or even demand a share of the profits generated from it.

- **Ethical and Humane Design:** Reimagined platforms would be designed not just for maximum engagement, but for human well-being. This is the core idea of the "humane technology" movement. In practice, this would mean designing for finitude, replacing the "infinite scroll" with clear stopping points. It would mean redesigning notification systems to be less intrusive and giving users more granular control. It would mean removing "vanity metrics" like public "like" counts that fuel social anxiety and performance. It would mean building in "friction," such as a mandatory pause before a user can share an article, giving them a moment to reflect on its veracity. These are not technologically difficult changes; they are simply contrary to the current business model.

- **A Fiduciary Duty of Care:** The most profound shift would be to move from the current legal paradigm of "terms of service" to a new paradigm of fiduciary duty. This would mean that platforms that hold vast amounts of personal data and mediate our access to information have a legal duty to act in the best interests of their users, much like a doctor, lawyer, or financial trustee. This single legal shift would make much of the current business model illegal. A platform with a fiduciary duty could not legally design an addictive interface, promote polarizing content to increase engagement, or sell access to their users' behavioral data to the highest bidder without explicit, informed, and uncoerced permission for a specific purpose. It would force a fundamental re-alignment of corporate interests with the public good.

Reimagining the State: From Doer to Enabler to Guardian

As discussed in the previous chapter, the role of the state must evolve from being a "doer" to a more sophisticated "enabler." But in the face of the challenges outlined in this book, even the "enabler" role is insufficient.

The state must assume two additional, critical roles for the digital age: Guardian of the Commons and Architect of Trust.

- **The Guardian of the Commons:** The digital public square is the new commons. Just as governments of the 20th century took on the role of protecting the physical environment from pollution and degradation, the 21st-century state must take on the role of protecting the digital environment. This means acting as a guardian against three primary threats.

    1. **Pollution:** The state must regulate the "informational pollution" of disinformation and hate speech, not through heavy-handed censorship, but through measures that increase platform liability and algorithmic transparency.

    2. **Enclosure:** The state must use robust antitrust and competition policy to prevent the "enclosure" of the commons by a few dominant monopolistic platforms, ensuring the market remains open and competitive.

    3. **Degradation:** The state must combat the general "degradation" of public discourse by investing in high-quality, non-commercial alternatives, such as public service media and civic technology platforms that are designed for deliberation, not outrage.

- **The Architect of Trust:** The state's most important role is to build the foundational layers of trust upon which a healthy digital ecosystem can flourish. Private innovation cannot solve this alone. The state must be the primary architect of the core infrastructure of trust. This includes establishing a secure, privacy-preserving, and citizen-controlled digital identity system. It involves setting and enforcing strong, clear data protection laws that give citizens meaningful rights over their personal information. It means driving the adoption of open standards and interoperability protocols that prevent vendor lock-in and ensure a level playing field. Without the state playing this role, the digital world will devolve into a chaotic and low-trust environment where only the largest and most powerful actors can thrive.

Part 3: The Leader's Playbook: A Detailed Call to Action

The path to a purposeful Digital Society requires more than just philosophy; it requires concrete and courageous action from national leaders.

Your journey as a leader is to navigate this complex terrain with wisdom and foresight.

The following principles are not simple instructions, but are expanded here into detailed policy briefs for the difficult work ahead.

1. Your Primary Challenge is Not Technological; It is Social

A thriving Digital Society is not an inevitable byproduct of technology deployment; it is a prerequisite for its success.

The most common and costly mistake leaders make is to focus on technology procurement while ignoring the social fabric.

A national strategy must begin with a deep investment in trust, literacy, and inclusion.

- **Actionable Policy Brief:** Launch a **National Digital Citizenship Strategy**. This would be a cross-government initiative with three pillars. First, a **nationwide digital literacy campaign**, run through schools, libraries, and public media, focused on the critical thinking and resilience skills needed to navigate the modern information environment. Second, the creation of an **Independent Media Fund**, publicly endowed but operationally independent, to support high-quality local journalism and investigative reporting, providing a trusted alternative to polluted social media feeds. Third, the establishment of **Citizen Assemblies on Technology**, where randomly selected groups of citizens are convened to deliberate on complex tech policy issues (like AI ethics or data privacy) and provide recommendations to parliament, thereby building public trust and legitimacy for difficult policy choices.

2. Define "Purpose" Through Negotiation, Not Declaration

Your guiding principle to be "PURPOSE DRIVEN" is correct, but in a democracy, purpose is always contested.

A top-down declaration of a singular national digital purpose, however well-intentioned, will be seen as authoritarian and will fail to achieve public buy-in.

Your role is not to impose a purpose, but to create a fair, transparent, and inclusive framework where competing interests can be negotiated.

- **Actionable Policy Brief:** Establish a **National Digital Council** by law. This would be a permanent, multi-stakeholder body tasked with advising the government on digital policy. Crucially, its membership must be legislated to include not just representatives from the tech industry and government ministries, but also from academia, trade unions, civil liberties groups, consumer advocates, and organizations representing marginalized communities. This council's deliberations and recommendations should be public by default, ensuring that the process of negotiating our digital future is done in the open.

3. Treat Private Platforms as Critical Infrastructure in Need of Regulation

The "Digital Town Square" is not a public space; it is a corporate one, and its architecture is designed for profit, not civic health.

Your government has a sovereign duty to mitigate the systemic harms these platforms can cause, from the spread of misinformation to the creation of algorithmic silos.

- **Actionable Policy Brief:** Introduce a landmark **Digital Services and Competition Act**. This legislation would have three core components. First, a **duty of care**, requiring platforms to take reasonable steps to mitigate foreseeable harms that can arise on their service, with significant penalties for failure. Second, **algorithmic transparency**, requiring major platforms to provide regulators and independent researchers with meaningful access to their data and models to audit for bias and systemic risks. Third, **pro-competitive measures**, such as mandating data portability and interoperability, to make it easier for users to switch services and for new, innovative competitors to emerge.

4. The "Enabler" Model Requires a Stronger, Not Weaker, Government

Shifting from a "doer" to an "enabler" is not about deregulation or stepping back; it is about developing new, more sophisticated state capacities.

The state must become a more intelligent referee, setting clear rules of the game, enforcing standards, and holding all actors, public and private, accountable to the public interest.

- **Actionable Policy Brief:** Launch a **21st-Century Civil Service Renewal Program**. This initiative would focus on building the internal capacities the state needs to be a smart enabler. This includes creating a dedicated **digital talent pipeline** to recruit top technologists into public service, reforming **government procurement processes** to be more agile and less risk-averse, and establishing a **national digital academy** to continuously upskill public servants in areas like data science, cybersecurity, and user-centric design.

5. Treat Citizen Data as Both a Sovereign Asset and a Profound Liability

Concepts like the Personal Profile Digital-Twin offer revolutionary potential for health and public service efficiency, but they also create catastrophic risks of data breaches and state surveillance.

The legal and security frameworks to protect this data are not an afterthought; they must be in place before such systems are built, not after a crisis.

- **Actionable Policy Brief:** Enact a **National Data and Digital Identity Act**. This law would establish a comprehensive data protection regime, similar to Europe's GDPR, based on the principles of data minimization, purpose limitation, and individual rights. It would also legally define the national digital identity model, enshrining principles of citizen control and privacy-by-design. Crucially, it would establish an independent, well-resourced **Data Protection Authority** with the power to conduct audits and impose significant fines, ensuring the law has teeth.

6. Use Technology to Fight Inequality, Not Amplify It

Left to market forces alone, technology will inevitably deepen the urban-rural divide and create a two-tiered education and health system.

Equity and inclusion cannot be assumed; they must be a conscious and deliberate design choice, embedded in every policy, every platform, and every procurement decision from the very beginning.

- **Actionable Policy Brief:** Implement a **National Digital Equity Agenda**. This would include a **Universal Service Fund** to aggressively subsidize broadband deployment in rural and underserved areas. It would legally mandate that all government digital services must meet the highest standards of **accessibility** for people with disabilities. And it would establish a **Public Interest Technology Fund** to invest in the creation of open-source educational software, assistive technologies, and civic platforms, ensuring that the benefits of technology are available to all, not just those who can afford premium services.

7. Embrace the "Brownfield"

The "greenfield country" is a useful thought experiment for clarifying vision, but you govern a complex "brownfield" of legacy systems, entrenched cultures, and powerful vested interests. Attempting a radical, top-to-bottom demolition of existing systems is politically naive and likely to fail.

True, lasting transformation is not achieved through revolution, but through persistent, intelligent, and strategic evolution.

- **Actionable Policy Brief:** Adopt a **Strategic Renovation Approach**. This means prioritizing ruthlessly. Identify a few high-impact, achievable projects that can deliver tangible value to citizens quickly, thereby building political capital and momentum for longer-term reforms. Create a "Legacy System Retirement Fund" to strategically decommission the most outdated and costly IT systems. Launch small-scale pilot projects and use their success stories to build a coalition for change. Celebrate the small wins, and understand that the work of transformation is a marathon, not a sprint.

Final Word: A Call to Courage

As a global society, we stand at a crossroads.

The choices we make today about how we design, regulate, and use technology will have consequences that reverberate for generations. We can choose to drift into a future where technology is seen merely as a tool for economic efficiency, for maximizing profit, and for exercising social control.

This is the path of least resistance.

It is the path of convenience.

Or, we can choose the more difficult path. We can choose to consciously and deliberately harness the immense power of these tools to build a more transparent, equitable, inclusive, and just world.

This choice is the central moral and ethical imperative of our time.

This is not a single choice to be made at a single moment. It is a series of continuous, small decisions made every day by software engineers writing code, by executives setting corporate policy, by legislators drafting laws, and by citizens deciding what to click on, what to share, and what to believe.

The imperative, therefore, is to make these myriad decision-making processes more transparent, more accountable, and more aligned with our highest public values.

We must embed our values—of fairness, privacy, dignity, and democracy—into the very architecture of our digital world.

If we are to avoid the dystopian pitfalls of unchecked surveillance, algorithmic bias, the erosion of privacy, and the decay of public discourse, we must be relentless in our pursuit of a purposeful Digital Society.

This requires more than just technological skill or political savvy; it requires moral courage.

It requires the courage to ask difficult questions, to challenge powerful interests, and to prioritize the long-term health of our society over the allure of short-term gains.

It requires a vision of a better, more honest, and more human future for all.

The work is unfinished.

Let us begin.

End Notes

This chapter lists sources for the specific data, examples, and concepts referenced in this book.

1. **Digital Twin Consortium**, What Is a Digital Twin?, accessed August 2, 2025, https://www.digitaltwinconsortium.org/hot-topics/digital-twins/; Synopsys, What is a Digital Twin?, accessed August 2, 2025, https://www.synopsys.com/glossary/what-is-a-digital-twin.html.
2. ITU, High-level Economic Study on the Impact of the Cost of International Internet Connectivity in Africa, accessed August 2, 2025, https://www.itu.int/en/ITU-D/Regulatory-Market/Pages/IIC_Africa_Study.aspx.
3. The World Bank, Mozambique Digital Acceleration Project, accessed August 2, 2025, https://documents.worldbank.org/en/publication/documents-reports/documentdetail/099333006282226593/p1777310dd2b8f0a008c2a0d7f4955c479e.
4. The Data Literacy Project, What is Data Literacy?, accessed August 2, 2025, https://thedataliteracyproject.org/what-is-data-literacy; National Association for Media Literacy Education, Media Literacy Defined, accessed August 2, 2025, https://namle.net/resources/media- literacy-defined/; National Cybersecurity Alliance, Cybersecurity Awareness, accessed August 2, 2025, https://staysafeonline.org/cybersecurity-awareness-month/.
5. UNESCO, Digital literacy in Africa, accessed August 2, 2025, https://www.unesco.org/en/articles/digital-literacy-africa.
6. USAID, Cameroon Digital Ecosystem Country Assessment & Honduras Digital Ecosystem Country Assessment, accessed August 2, 2025, https://www.usaid.gov/digital-

development/digital-ecosystem-country-assessments.
7. United Nations, E-Government Development Index (EGDI), accessed August 2, 2025, https://publicadministration.un.org/egovkb/en-us/About/UNeGDI.
8. Jisc, *Exploring digital wellbeing*, accessed August 2, 2025, https://www.jisc.ac.uk/guides/exploring-digital-wellbeing.
9. GSMA, The Mobile Gender Gap Report 2024, accessed August 2, 2025, https://www.gsma.com/mobilefordevelopment/resources/the-mobile-gender-gap-report-2024/.
10. European Commission, eGovernment Benchmark 2023, accessed August 2, 2025, https://digital-strategy.ec.europa.eu/en/news/egovernment-benchmark-2023-digital-government-services-europe-improve-are-not-yet-seamless-across.
11. McCrindle Research, Understanding Generation Z, accessed August 2, 2025, https://mccrindle.com.au/article/topic/generation-z/understanding-generation-z/.
12. OECD, Recommendation of the Council on Open Government, accessed August 2, 2025, https://legalinstruments.oecd.org/en/instruments/OECD-LEGAL-0438.
13. United Nations, E-Government Survey 2022, accessed August 2, 2025, https://publicadministration.un.org/egovkb/en-us/reports/un-e-government-survey-2022.
14. The Official Website of Denmark, Digital Denmark, accessed August 2, 2025, https://denmark.dk/innovation-and-design/digital-denmark.
15. e-Estonia, e-Voting, accessed August 2, 2025, https://e-estonia.com/solutions/e-governance/i-voting/.
16. Gov.uk, Local digital case study: South Korea, accessed August 2, 2025, https://www.gov.uk/government/publications/local-digital-case-studies/local-digital-case-study-south-korea.
17. Ministry of Digital Transformation of Ukraine, Diia, accessed August 2, 2025, https://thedigital.gov.ua/diia.
18. Centre for Public Impact, How a crisis spurred Ukraine's digital

transformation, accessed August 2, 2025, https://www.centreforpublicimpact.org/insights/field-notes/how-crisis-spurred-ukraines-digital-transformation.

19. OECD, Digital Government Review of San Marino, accessed August 2, 2025, https://www.oecd.org/gov/digital-government-review-of-san-marino-739b6b72-en.htm.
20. BDO, Digital Transformation in Kuwait, accessed August 2, 2025, https://www.bdo.com.kw/en-gb/insights/2024/digital-transformation-in-kuwait-navigating-the-future-of-business.
21. Interpol, African Cybercrime Report 2022, accessed August 2, 2025, https://www.interpol.int/en/News-and-Events/News/2022/Africa-s-cybercrime-landscape-and-the-policing-response.
22. Access Now, Myanmar: The international community must stop the junta's digital coup, accessed August 2, 2025, https://www.accessnow.org/press-release/myanmar-junta-digital-coup/.
23. The World Bank, Excellence in Digital Education, accessed August 2, 2025, https://www.worldbank.org/en/topic/edutech/brief/excellence-in-digital-education.
24. Smart Nation Singapore, Smart Nation: The Way Forward, & European Commission, Finland's Digital Compass, accessed August 2, 2025, https://www.smartnation.gov.sg/about-smart-nation/the-way-forward and https://digital-strategy.ec.europa.eu/en/policies/finlands-digital-compass.
25. UNICEF, Syrian Arab Republic: Education, accessed August 2, 2025, https://www.unicef.org/syria/education.
26. European Commission, Europe's Digital Decade: digital targets for 2030, accessed August 2, 2025, https://commission.europa.eu/strategy-and-policy/priorities-2019-2024/europe-fit-digital-age/europes-digital-decade-digital-targets-2030_en.
27. Cedefop, Skills shortages and surpluses in European labour markets, accessed August 2, 2025, https://www.cedefop.europa.eu/en/publications/9172.
28. SkillsFuture Singapore, SkillsFuture, accessed August 2, 2025, https://www.skillsfuture.gov.sg/.

29. The World Bank, Digital Nigeria: A comprehensive diagnostic of the digital economy, accessed August 2, 2025, https://www.worldbank.org/en/country/nigeria/publication/digital-nigeria-a-comprehensive-diagnostic-of-the-digital-economy.
30. The Asia Foundation, In Nepal, A Digital Skills Gap Hampers a Generation, accessed August 2, 2025, https://asiafoundation.org/2023/08/23/in-nepal-a-digital-skills-gap-hampers-a-generation/.
31. Saudi Press Agency, Seha Virtual Hospital Performs Over 6,000 Successful Surgeries, accessed August 2, 2025, https://www.spa.gov.sa/en/N1962322.
32. Center for Global Development, Togo's NOVISSI: A Digital G2P Payment Case Study, accessed August 2, 2025, https://www.cgdev.org/publication/togos-novissi-digital-g2p-payment-case-study.
33. The World Bank, Digital Cash Transfers in Haiti, accessed August 2, 2025, https://www.worldbank.org/en/news/feature/2023/03/23/haiti-digital-cash-transfers-provide-lifeline-for-vulnerable-families.
34. The Economic Times, More than 815 million Indian citizens' data exposed in massive breach, & Bangkok Post, 9m patient records leaked, accessed August 2, 2025, https://economictimes.indiatimes.com/tech/technology/over-800-million-indian-citizens-personal-data-leaked-from-icmr-database/articleshow/104686001.cms and https://www.bangkokpost.com/thailand/general/2642503.
35. Oxford Business Group, How Ghana is working to close the digital divide, accessed August 2, 2025, https://oxfordbusinessgroup.com/reports/ghana/2023-report/ict/how-ghana-is-working-to-close-the-digital-divide/.
36. The World Bank, Pakistan: Digital Economy Diagnostic, accessed August 2, 2025, https://thedocs.worldbank.org/en/doc/182411634515554799-0090022021/original/Pakistan-DECA-Main-Report-100621.pdf.
37. InnovandoPY, Official Website, accessed August 2, 2025, https://www.innovando.gov.py/.
38. Digital Belgium, Official Website, accessed August 2, 2025, https://www.digitalbelgium.be/en.

39. Nordic Institute for Interoperability Solutions, X-Road®, accessed August 2, 2025, https://x-road.global/.
40. Zipline, "Delivering for Rwanda," accessed August 2, 2025, https://www.flyzipline.com/rwanda.
41. NHS, "The NHS App," accessed August 2, 2025, https://www.nhs.uk/nhs-app/.
42. BBC News, "Cyber-attack on HSE: What we know so far," May 20, 2021, https://www.bbc.com/news/world-europe-57150579.
43. Foucault, Michel. Discipline and Punish: The Birth of the Prison. Vintage Books, 1995. (For concepts of Panopticon and Biopower).
44. Bradford, Anu. The Brussels Effect: How the European Union Rules the World. Oxford University Press, 2020.
45. Digital 9, "The Charter of the Digital 9," accessed August 2, 2025, https://www.d9.ee/charter/.
46. GovStack, "GovStack Initiative," accessed August 2, 2025, https://www.govstack.global/.
47. Caulfield, Mike. "SIFT (The Four Moves)," accessed August 2, 2025, https://hapgood.us/sift-the-four-moves/.
48. Hirsch Jr., E.D. Cultural Literacy: What Every American Needs to Know. Vintage, 1988.
49. PISA (Programme for International Student Assessment), "PISA 2022 Results," OECD, accessed August 2, 2025, https://www.oecd.org/pisa/results/.
50. Bourdieu, Pierre. "The Forms of Capital." In Handbook of Theory and Research for the Sociology of Education, edited by John G. Richardson, 241-258. Greenwood Press, 1986.
51. Beauchamp, Tom L., and James F. Childress. Principles of Biomedical Ethics. 8th ed. Oxford University Press, 2019.

www.ingramcontent.com/pod-product-compliance
Lightning Source LLC
Chambersburg PA
CBHW041300210926
51847CB00009B/91
9789699092022